POLARIZING AMERICA

A Dichotomous Society

RANDY PURHAM

Published by Bombardier Books
An Imprint of Post Hill Press

ISBN: 979-8-89565-404-0
ISBN (eBook): 979-8-89565-405-7

Polarizing America:
A Dichotomous Society

Cover Design by Jim Villaflores

This is a work of nonfiction. All people, locations, events, and situations are portrayed to the best of the author's memory.

This book, as well as any other Bombardier Books publications, may be purchased in bulk quantities at a special discounted rate. Contact orders@bombardierbooks.com for more information.

Post Hill Press
New York • Nashville
posthillpress.com

Published in the United States of America
1 2 3 4 5 6 7 8 9 10

CONTENTS

PREFACE

IN THIS BOOK, I WANTED to express my (unique) views, thoughts, and sentiments about a myriad of topics especially in the realm of social justice, politics, and just living in America. *Polarizing America* will lay out the various issues that have transpired and that are currently ongoing in American society through a few lenses: the media lens, the lens of reality and history, and the lens of societal perspective and reaction. Virtually everything is now a political movement sparked by emotions and money. What sells and sensationalizes the masses is what dominates the news cycle and the trending topics on the various social media platforms; never mind if it's true. Let us not forget that everyone is a political and social pundit or expert in the social media world as well. Everything in life has evolved into emoticons, emojis, memes, and hashtags. Once again, spurned by feelings/emotions, perspectives, and what we choose to empathize with for the moment—whether the week or a few months. The real causes that sparked true civil unrest are long gone, and people have grown to protest any and everything out of sheer boredom—not that they actually care. More often than not, they were paid to do so. Americans seem to fail to understand that we, as a collective society, are enduring a lot of issues that the rest of the world has already dealt with or may be going through presently themselves, but have it figured out. We are literally the "social infants of the world" and the rest are sitting back and watching us with the expression of "Aww, that's cute!"

If you are looking for a politically correct and sensitively cognitive read, put this down and walk away. I will likely piss you off or you may disagree with me on a lot of points. That is perfectly okay. I never expect people to agree with me or acknowledge that I am correct. That is based on a series of things. I am what you may call a "Black Unicorn." I am a conservative who happens to believe in the Constitution, Conservative values and principles, capitalism, and Christianity—who happens to be Black (African American), Person of Color, or whatever label fits your particular social construct. To put it more directly: I am a Republican Black Man! Cue: RUN!!! If you are ready for a power-packed read, then sit back with your drink of choice or favorite playlist and enjoy. I appreciate you coming this far and will appreciate it more if you continue your journey through this book to get an outside-the-box view of American society and how we can collectively overcome our challenges.

INTRODUCTION

THE AMERICAN POLITICAL SYSTEM IS not a strange or difficult one for one to process or understand. There are two dominant parties—Republicans and Democrats. Yes, there are a lot of other parties or "sub-parties." The Independent Party is a growing party; but one can reasonably say that you will not see any significant movement from that party for years to come. I'll cover that part in the next chapter. The various parties and sub-parties have their causes and reasons as to why they exist. I will not go into all of them or the whys and hows, but I will touch on a few things. The Grand Old Party (GOP), formally known as the Republican Party, is by far the most stable party compared to the Democratic and Independent parties. Often called the "right-wing" party, it is not coincidental as to why. Republicans are also considered, or mostly called, Conservatives because they believe in gradual change. Once, that aligned with the idea of being progressive—but holistically, they lean toward keeping things the same or at least in a traditional sense. The idea that "If it's not broken, don't fix it" is the best way to identify a Conservative.

The Democratic Party has been around since the better part of the mid-1700s. They often change platforms and parts of their planks to appease what is popular for the duration—this happens about every twenty to thirty years. The Independent Party sprung up in the late 1960s, and I jokingly call them the "Indecisive Party." The IP prides itself on being a party of independent thinkers, apart from the ideologies and principles of the two currently established parties—more like being a mixed bag of marbles. However, they often pick and choose from both sides to build their narrative (platform) and just word it differently. You really cannot have a third opinion—I often say this; therefore, we have two sides to a lot of things in life. The left side of the brain and the right side of the brain is a prime example. But make no mistake, they are still part of one body. As most people put it today: "The left wing and the right wing; still part of the same bird!" Absolutely!

Most modern-day Republicans are Constitutionalist, Conservative-principled, Christian-centered, and Capitalist-based—mostly, that is. There are factions that trickle into the party that are called RINOs (Republican in name only) that say they are Republicans, but do or say opposite of what Republicans traditionally stand for (see the four Cs above). Oftentimes, people associate the GOP as the party for old racist white people—which couldn't be further from the truth. And please save the argument that the party switched sides. No, the parties shifted in planks and saw that some things were not a necessity to have as a cause anymore—nationally that is. This shift began in the late 1950s. That is not switching sides; that is changing focus or direction. Notably, some Republicans began changing their party views going back to the days of Truman's administration as the country began to emerge from World War II. The idea of a strong defense system gave rise to the military-industrial complex that proceeded after President Eisenhower—which he warned about.[1] I ask this question quite often: At what party convention did the Republicans and Democrats switch platforms? Better yet, during

1 "The Great Switch: How the Republican & Democratic Parties Flipped Ideologies," Students of History, 2023, https://www.studentsofhistory.com/ideologies-flip-Democratic-Republican-parties.

what session of Congress did the Speaker say "Okay, you guys over here, and you guys go over there—we're switching sides!"?

If you were to divide the United States into a "quintant"—five political categories—you'd find that there are varying ideologies and beliefs influencing a person's decision to say that they are "X-Party." Other parties and sub-parties adopted planks of their own as a "pseudo-ideology" just to garner more financial support, votes, and power. Now, impartially speaking, *all* political parties have done this to a degree, that is, steal from each other. It's called being a politician. As we go through the following chapters, I will explain this in greater detail.

The Democratic Party has been deemed the party for minorities—although it's driven by white Democrats.... Strangely, this party plays into a lot of the social issues that are popular for the time being without exercising any true legislation to support these various causes—not any that are long-term or meaningful, anyway. What comes to mind: The Commission to Study Reparations[2] (more on that later). Democrats have always put up policies or legislation aimed to fix "a problem," but these very policies typically exacerbate the problems or don't address them at all—the Inflation Reduction Act[3] is one example—just Band-Aids to cover an amputation. There are many conservative-minded minorities that occupy the Democratic Party—we call them DINOs (Democrats in name only). Similarly to the RINOs, DINOs do and say things that are more in line with Republican views but claim to be Democrats. I believe this is more for the purpose of

2 US Congress, Commission to Study Reparations, Congress.gov, 2023, https://www.congress.gov/bill/118th-congress/senate-bill/40?q=%7B%22search%22%3A%22Commission+to+study+reparations%22%7D&s=2&r=1.

3 US Congress, Inflation Reduction Act, Congress.gov, 2023, https://www.congress.gov/bill/118th-congress/house-bill/812?q=%7B%22search%22%3A%22Inflation+Reduction+Act%22%7D&s=1&r=2.

social acceptance than a reason of personal principle or supporting party platforms that they actually believe in. I've had many conversations with minority Democrats, and the numbers are overwhelmingly in opposition to actually advocating and supporting the party platform. This boils down to generational voting in many cases. Case in point, there are many minorities that identify and may even vote Republican in a primary election, but will not openly admit or own that they are a Republican for the mere fact that it's traditionally unacceptable—especially in the Black community—to be a Republican. This goes back to the "switching sides" notion—"The parties switched and so should you!" The Democratic Party is a great party for those who cherish a few key things: inner city life, government assistance or subsidies, and socializing the free market so everyone can achieve—I mean benefit—even at the expense of eliminating a more successful entity from the equation.

Liberals and Progressives are your main occupiers of the Democratic Party; their ideology and politics sit on the left or far left—depending on the issue. To many Americans, the Left's ideology, platform, and planks seem absurd, or just simply a nuance to what most consider middle-of-the-road principles. You will rarely, if ever, find an activist or protest movement that is not Democratic in nature. The Right often feels that these are a waste and would rather discuss or legislate the issue at hand. At the same time, however, Republican activism does look similar but is executed differently in terms of action items taken. (At the time of this writing in 2018, that was the case. The Trump Era brought a different brand of activism and movements to the political arena, which I will discuss in greater detail later.)

Let's now look at the quintant of the political map in the US, as I alluded to earlier. Northwestern states, Southwestern states,

Mid-America, Northeastern states, and Southeastern states—all have their own set of collective intra-geopolitical voting interests, and then it trickles into their individual interests based on their location and lifestyle. For quick examples: Northwestern interests currently tend to center around marijuana use, climate change, and LBGTQ(IA+) issues. Southwestern interests are predominantly around border security, abortion rights, and election integrity. Mid-America interests usually focus on land development, inner-city (urban) matters, and economic growth as well as the Dakota Access Pipeline and the Keystone Pipeline—notably, since the election of President Joe Biden, permit renewals for the Keystone Pipeline project have been eliminated.[4] Northeastern interests are typically around environmental and industrial issues (steel, coal, and manufacturing). Southeastern interests are more commonly revolving around civil rights of LBGTQ(IA) issues—since they are in the "Bible Belt"—along with abortion rights. This is not to say other states or areas are not facing some of the same issues, but it is to say that is what dominates the local news cycle for these areas. There are a myriad of other associated issues within each individual quintant. As we progress through this book, they will be covered in more detail.

Allow me to refer you to some additional reading: The Republican Party Platforms of 2016 and 2020, and the Democratic Party Platforms of 2016 and 2020. Read them both and do an actual comparison of their agendas and ideologies. Each party revises their platforms and agendas about every four years—based on presidencies and the societal tidal waves of issues. Both platforms can be found in a simple Google/Bing search. Another book to assist in checking your azimuth on the political spectrum is *You Know You're a Republican/Democrat If...* by Frank Benjamin. This

4 Melissa Denchak and Courtney Lindwall, "What Is the Keystone XL Pipeline?" January 30, 2025, NRDC, https://www.nrdc.org/stories/what-keystone-xl-pipeline#whatis.

book goes point by point in short bursts to give you indicators—mostly in a comedic way—on how you can determine whether you are a Republican or a Democrat. For example: You know you're a Republican if you are afraid of the IRS. You know you're a Democrat if you are afraid of the FBI.[5] Packed with stereotyping, it plays into those talking points of each of the major political parties. After all, stereotypes are derived from some truths, right? As we traverse through this chapter and the rest of the book, you will notice how the parties didn't switch sides—they just merely evolved in ideologies and shifted focus onto other developing issues. When I hear that the parties switched sides, I ask people: "So did the parties come into their chambers in a new session and say, 'Hey you all! You come on this side and be called Democrats now, and we'll come over there and be called Republicans!'?" That is absurd! What did happen is that some members of Congress didn't like the way their party was changing and figured they could use their influence and power to sway others or continue their "ways" by simply switching parties. I will note that in my opinion, President Lyndon Baines Johnson (LBJ) did have a genuine heart to change and provide equality across America. However, I do also believe there were some unintended consequences that went along with his policies, and most "older southern Democrats" took advantage of those policies and opportunities to advance their own agendas and saw it as a paradigm-shifting opportunity to garner minority supporters. The Great Society was notably the most damaging policy eras for minorities—specifically Blacks/African Americans—during the 1960s through present day. The Civil Rights Act (CRA) of '64 were great steps toward establishing equality among the races in America, but what ensued afterwards unraveled the intent—arguably, unintended consequences

5 Frank Benjamin, *You Know You're a Republican/Democrat If...* 2016, Sourcebooks.

of those laws. The CRA was reluctantly passed in the House and viciously fought in the Senate, where Senator Everett Dirksen (R-IL) ultimately "whipped" the bill into passage. I will not go into the long drawn out history of what happened and when. Just understand that a series of things transpired through the late '60s and '70s, and even a few events in the '80s, that brought us to the status quo of the "Urban America" of today.

At the time of writing this book (2018), these are the hottest national issues that are election topics and on legislative agendas: abortion, repeal of the Affordable Care Act (ACA or "Obamacare"), same-sex marriage, defunding of Planned Parenthood, the border wall, Common Core, and tax cuts/plan. I will discuss these in minor detail. Picking back up in this book in 2021, I will now provide a sense of updates throughout—I won't go back and change anything, as I want to illustrate the transhistorical changes that have occurred in the three short years that I have been working on this book. I've completed the core of this book in October 2023.

Author's note: While this book has been in the works since 2018, I have picked back up in doing some revisions and additions throughout in 2025 as I am now finally preparing it for publication. It remains vital to highlight the changes in the political landscape over the last seven years as this book's intended purpose is to serve as a brief history lesson of recent and not-so-distant past events.

▪ CHAPTER 1 ▪

PLATFORMS AND PLANKS OF AMERICAN POLITICS

ABORTION

One of the most divisive issues in America today is abortion—barring what stage of abortion. Among Republicans, it's a matter of religious principle to be "pro-life." Along with that comes personal responsibility and accountability for one's actions. Among Democrats, it's a matter of personal choice: "pro-choice." Women have a right to choose, and it's their body, burden, and decision. Both sides arguably make great points, and I have had great debates on the matter. I would like to point out a few things that may prompt you and others to think about some things about abortion.

> Should an individual/couple partake in an activity (sex), produce a child, and she or they decide to not have the baby? Is it incumbent upon others to pay for an abortion via taxpayer dollars? Or do we encourage personal responsibility in practicing safe sex or implement control measures to prevent an unwanted pregnancy? Is it truly just the woman's decision to carry a child or does the father have a say in the matter too? Who deems that the child is not a human being until birth? Why is having a

baby a matter of choice, but having sex isn't—especially if you're not in a position to take care of a child? Would it be better to place the child for adoption or seek assistance from family and friends in helping raise the child?

Sure, these are all conservative viewpoints in the matter, but does it not make sense? I look at this issue from both a conservative standpoint as well as a racial one. African Americans (Blacks) make up 13.7 percent of the US population, or roughly forty-one million people.[6] Planned Parenthood (a facility that provides medical services such as breast cancer screenings, drug addiction counseling, and other family support services, but has its notoriety from providing abortions) facilities are most notably and mainly established in minority (Black) communities, thus contributing to the low population rate of the African Americans in the US. Is it by design? Is it intentional? I will point you in the direction of Margaret Sanger, founder of Planned Parenthood; you could ask her yourself—if she were alive—but since she's deceased, you can research her position on the matter yourself.[7] Also, it is most notable that this is a government-funded program, advocated by the Democratic Party. You would think that people would connect the dots and see the systematic destructive mechanism in place. But it is pawned off as a service so desperately needed in minority communities because they cannot afford or have access to healthcare. This leads into my next agenda-based item: defunding Planned Parenthood. For obvious reasons, the Republicans want to defund Planned Parenthood and consoli-

6 US Census Bureau, Population: Quick Facts, 2024, https://www.census.gov/quickfacts/fact/table/US/RHI225223.

7 Comcast Corporation v. National Association of African American–Owned Media, et al., No.18-1171, (2019), https://www.supremecourt.gov/DocketPDF/18/18-1171/116542/20190920143641893_18-1171%20Amicus%20Brief%20of%20ISSUES4LIFE%20Foundation.pdf.

date the resources in more pragmatic settings—actual clinics and hospitals. This approach I support because, if access is granted or made easier under the provisions of the ACA, then what is the issue with consolidating these services into clinics and hospitals? Affordability and transportability should not be a factor in this case.

I won't get into the religious aspects of abortion because (1) there are varying biblical perspectives about abortion, (2) that will require a whole different book to accommodate all the religions out there and their views about abortion—not to mention the internal varying interpretations of the matter, and (3) a lot of people who may be in support of abortion rights—whatever that may look like—are not affiliated to any religion. So, to my fellow Republicans, telling someone what the Bible says...when they clearly are not a Christian or of religious sorts is basically pointless.... Find a new persuasive argument that will resonate with those opposing your viewpoint. Such as the responsibility approach, or *don't have recreational sex that will lead to recreational abortion*. That one is my personal favorite argument.

HEALTHCARE

Repealing the ACA is one of the campaign promises that President Donald Trump made—as had many other Republicans who were running for office or have since been elected. The ACA was designed to provide affordable healthcare to all Americans and establishes exchanges and subsidies to help offset costs to middle- and lower-income families and individuals. This is a huge plus for some middle-income and no-income families. I won't go into the ins and outs of ACA and who it benefits and does not. The key takeaway that affects nearly all Americans is the "mandate" portion. The mandate penalizes those who do not have a medical insurance plan approved by, or that meets the criteria outlined in, the ACA.[8] There are families that face paying hundreds of dollars a month for coverage or risk a stiff penalty come tax season that runs into the thousands. Two close friends of mine divulged that they were smacked with a $3,000 fine. But neither held a job long enough throughout the year to afford the payments—nor did they even use the services. Republicans see this as a flaw and an underhanded way to get people to pay into a system or pay the government if they failed to do so. Democrats have advocated for the necessary evil and sacrifice Americans will make for the betterment of the less fortunate. (Sounds like Communism to me….) The issue I take with the mandate is that this disproportionately affects middle-to-upper-income families in forcing them to pay for something through monthly payments or face a penalty via their taxes—which most families rely on to help recover from the holiday spending. In 2017, President Trump got rid of the ACA mandate—one of his key victories with a Republican-controlled Congress. While it didn't go into effect until 2019, it proved to be a financial relief to many families and a legislative win for the Trump administration. However, on the flipside, California is one of the few states that still implements this penalty clause at the state level—go figure!

8 Christine Eibner and Sarah Nowak, "The Effect of Eliminating the Individual Mandate Penalty and the Role of Behavioral Factors," The Commonwealth Fund, July 11, 2018, https://www.commonwealthfund.org/publications/fund-reports/2018/jul/eliminating-individual-mandate-penalty-behavioral-factors.

SAME-SEX MARRIAGE

Another heartfelt burning issue in America is same-sex marriage. For centuries, the standing tradition and recognized practice in marriage was and has been between one man and one woman. I personally have mixed feelings about the issue, but I will put it as plain as this. Not everyone carries a religious sentiment or ideology; therefore, laws and prohibitions should not be guided or enforced on the basis of religion alone. With that being said, I view marriage as a common union between two human beings—a biological man and a biological woman.

Whether it's between man and woman, woman and woman, man and four men, man and four women, or a woman and three men, it's their personal business and as long as it does not infringe on or affect the livelihood of day-to-day business and order of others, who should really give a damn? I find that is the Libertarian side of me coming out there, but seriously—who cares? However, that is me! Marriage has always been universally and religiously defined as given previously; all other relationship types and arrangements should be recognized as they are and given titles of civil unions, not marriage, because laws and traditions that may recognize those things are just that—recognition, not the right to usurp and corrupt the term "marriage." Democrats, on the other hand, believe the philosophy that people should be able to marry whomever they choose and love—growing in that sentiment are children and animals—I'm not kidding.[9] [10]

9 "California Democrats Protect Offenders Who Lure Minors," California Senate Republicans, February 19, 2019, https://src.senate.ca.gov/content/california-democrats-protect-offenders-who-lure-minors.

10 Ryan Farmer, "2022 House Bill 209: Maryland Democrats Seek to Legalize Acts of Bestiality." *The News and Times,* January 17, 2022, https://www.newsandtimes.com/politics/2022/01/2022-house-bill-209-maryland-democrats-seek-to-legalize-acts-of-bestiality/.

Republicans feel that the institution of marriage is a sacred one and should not be exploited or compromised with the ungodly and forbidden union between two people of the same sex or of different species for that matter. Although we are in new times and things are progressively changing, that is a view I can personally stand by and would expect those who are in practice of the Christian faith to adhere to as well. However, I also believe that we should not impose our beliefs onto those who do not believe in or practice what Christians do. The best practice—I feel—is to just take marital control away from the government. Period. If two people or more want to consider themselves "married" or in a "civil union," they may do so with contracts and a notary and move on. Ceremonies and recognition will be a private matter (friends-and-family type of thing). Simple as that. Now, some will say, what about taxes and estate issues? Well, that goes back to a contract or any other court-recognized document that spells it out to determine those affairs. Change the tax codes to "filing-jointly" (remove "married") and keep it simple. I think we overcomplicate certain things in our society just for the sake of job security or to sound smart. This falls in line with Bureaucracy 101.

Some Americans will lead you to believe that there is an element of the law called "separation of church and state," and that "we are not a country founded on religious principles." Both are false narratives and very far from the truth. "Separation of church and state" clearly and solely references the letter by Thomas Jefferson in 1802 to the Danbury Baptist Association, citing his views and further explaining the constitutional provision that the government shall not interfere with how a religious institution practices its faith, prohibit the practice of its religion, nor establish a national religion—"thus building a wall of separation between church and state."[11] Recognizing these important words and understanding the implications of religion mixed into governing a nation, the Founding Fathers intentionally left religion covertly and, in some instances, overtly out of the process of drafting the government and founding the United States. All of the signers of the Declaration of Independence came from various religious backgrounds, and some even held various degrees in Freemasonry, as well as positions in public and professional services. They knew the importance of not establishing a religion but extracting some of the common and natural (God's) laws and practices that would promote good order and discipline among the citizens and this "new nation."

BORDER SECURITY

Moving on to the border wall—one of President Trump's biggest campaign promises and the bane of existence for every sitting president since Andrew Jackson. This particular issue sits near and dear to the hearts of the Southwestern citizens, but holistically affects every American. Illegal immigration has been a problem in this country for decades. I capitalized Illegal because immigrants who come through proper legal and documented channels are at least in a recognized system; they have documentation and WE know who they are, where they come from, and, for the most part, where they are going or will be going. And typically, they are welcomed into the communities in which they choose to settle.

Illegal immigrants, on the other hand, sneak into the country unidentified, having no [proper] documentation, using human

11 "Jefferson's Letter to the Danbury Baptists: Final Letter, as Sent," Library of Congress, 1802, https://www.loc.gov/loc/lcib/9806/danpre.html.

resources, possibly committing crimes (that potentially go unsolved), work American jobs and send the money back home out of the United States, apply for government assistance or use public programs for their benefit, vote illegally in our elections, engage in human child/sex trafficking, and the list goes on and on. I'm sure you get my drift. This actually isn't my drift; these are the plights and issues that we are faced with when dealing with the illegal immigration crisis. In 2015 and 2016, we had the migrant caravan coming to the southern border to seek refugee status and enter the United States as asylum seekers. President Trump cut a deal with Mexico to keep the caravan there, and they bi-laterally worked to identify those with legitimate claims and ensure that they were properly processed before entering the country.[12]

In 2021, the migrant caravan reemerged with promises and assistance from the Biden administration to usher in these migrants and grant them amnesty into the country to the tune of eleven million additional folks, all the while halting border wall construction, sending money to South American countries for aid and support to these caravans, and halting the deportation program.

Border protection and security should not be a matter of question or debate. The reasons mentioned above should be sufficient to garner national and collective support to put up funding and the materials necessary to prevent illegal immigration. We can look at Canada's border protection as an example. They have checkpoints at points of entry and gates with patrols in areas less traveled. When someone crosses into Canada, they are immediately apprehended. In other countries, illegal crossing is consid-

12 Muzaffar Chishti and Jessica Bolter, "Remain in Mexico Plan Echoes Earlier U.S. Policy to Deter Haitian Migration," Migration Policy Institute, March 28, 2019, https://www.migrationpolicy.org/article/remain-mexico-plan-echoes-earlier-us-policy-deter-haitian-migration.

ered trespassing and death is the potential result. I think we can all agree that having secured borders for the protection of citizens and resources is pretty reasonable. People on the Left who advocate for open borders are typically unaffected by it and have not analyzed or seen the implications of such matters. Sure, we are a country of immigrants; sure, this country was taken from Natives in a not-so-distant past; sure, we are an open, loving, and tolerant nation. However, I still want to know who you are. Let's visit this subject on a micro scale.

> Let's say you have a home of your own. You leave for the day/night and you leave your doors and windows unlocked. (Don't worry, you're a liberal. You support open borders and a welcoming society, so it's okay to leave these things unsecured.) You come home to find strangers occupying your home, eating your food, lying in your bed, using your shower, wearing your clothes. (You know, all the things you worked for.) What would you do? How would you feel? Remember, your home is a free, open, and welcoming place. Never did you think in a million years that you would be occupied by a force in numbers.

That is exactly how most Americans feel about illegal immigrants on a macro scale. Is it fair or even appropriate that someone comes into your house, occupies it at will, and uses your resources, even though you didn't invite them, know who they are, where they came from, or even why they are there—unannounced no less?

EDUCATION

Perhaps the United States' education system is a little more of a concern for you. Here is a quick Google search definition of what Common Core is, for those unfamiliar—whether due to not having school-aged children or because you simply never cared. The Common Core State Standards Initiative is an educational initiative in the United States that details what K-12 students should know in English language arts and mathematics at the end of each grade. The initiative is sponsored by the National Governors Association (NGA) and the Council of Chief State School Officers (CCSSO) and seeks to establish consistent educational standards across the states as well as ensure that students graduating from high school are prepared to enter credit-bearing courses at two- or four-year college programs or to enter the workforce.[13]

First off, who in hell died and made you "Emperor of Education" to tell me what my child(ren) should know by a certain grade?! I fully understand the consequence of sending your child to public education institutions: You are at the mercy of such tomfoolery. But still…a board, group, panel, body—whomever—came together and laid out a set ideas, topics, and subjects to be universally taught across the board. Here's where the problem with this lies. Children in the same grade level have various learning needs and attention levels. Some teachers will argue that they teach according to those demands—others, not so much. In this arena, Common Core has given teachers/students "packets" with information to be taught, length of time, and objectives to achieve by the end of the "module." This gives

13 "Frequently Asked Questions," Common Core Standards States Initiative, 2012, https://web.archive.org/web/20140226221237/http://www.corestandards.org/resources/frequently-asked-questions.

little to no room for expansion or creative thinking and teaching because they are confined to the materials given.

I've had several heated discussions with quite a few friends of mine that are in this profession, and they beg to differ. They mostly stated that they are free to teach whatever they wish out of the topic. They can use additional materials or sources. They may be confined to that area, but they can expand to tie into the next lesson, and so on. All of these are hopefully true in their respective cases. But, from what I have witnessed and had to deal with in my children's education (mind you, across three different states since 2009) is that they are given a syllabus—in most classes—and a bunch of handouts for both home and class to use for the term. I can't recall seeing a textbook in a very long time, except for a few of the high school classes. Granted, it's 2017, and classes are moving into the digital age of tablets and laptops as their source of learning—but, my GOD! I'm all for some programs to be universal or standardized across the country—like teaching basic US history, government/civics, English (speaking, reading, and writing), and math. These are things that affect every person in our society on a daily basis, and the lack of knowledge and understanding of these basics is staggering.

Some scholars would argue that that is the goal and is what is being done in Common Core. If that was the case, then we would not see the disparities across the country that we do. So, where is the failure at? I fully support the STEM (science, technology, engineering, and mathematics) initiative and programs of higher education/learning. I also feel that such programs—if offered in regular schools—should be classified as elective-based curriculum. Education in the public school system should be structured and goal-oriented to age- and grade-appropriate levels. Parents and teachers should work together with students to not only teach, but mold and foster them into being productive members of society on the basis of certain foundations that are mutually agreeable and achievable for that child. Rarely—if ever—does the "cookie-cutter" method work in education. It works in the workforce and the military—to an extent—but teaching children requires a special skill set, and the understanding that everyone learns differently and has different learning needs is paramount. One child may not excel in math, but can structure a paragraph better than the editor in chief of a newspaper. Skill sets like this should be honed, sharpened, and cultivated for the child and society at large.

Please do not get me wrong. I can understand the Liberal ideology behind wanting to make education equal across the spectrum of the US, but there has to be and will be differences in education in some aspects—geographically speaking. Like I mentioned previously, not everyone is STEM-oriented or STEM material, and we have a severe lack of understanding of basic subjects in our society in the areas of reading, math, science, and especially history (including civics and social studies). I think the elementary school years should focus on these areas, and then high school should introduce a more "adult-life focused" curriculum (including life skills such as banking, taxes, buying cars, homes, renting, raising a family, running a business, and getting into politics), and STEM programs. Finally, the college circuit can be focused on honing the skills, knowledge, and attributes of these special industries and professions, such as those in STEM fields.

TAXES AND JOBS

Finally, the Tax Cuts and Jobs Act, congressionally known as H.R.1, was passed a few days before Christmas of 2017.[14] The US income tax system hasn't seen an overhaul of this magnitude since 1986. I will be one of many to say that it was long overdue, mainly because of the economic landscape changes that have taken place over the years. Things cost more, people are making more money, and global competition in terms of technology, innovation, job growth, and manufacturing are on a steady rise. We, in the United States, have a pretty high corporate tax rate—35 percent—in comparison to many other countries with 21–25 percent. The reduction in the corporate tax rate will entice businesses to stay in the US and not take their flagships elsewhere. This will also lead to job growth and economic growth. But many don't see it that way. Those who are opposed to the tax bill see it as a payday for the rich or a boost for them to keep more money. Well, in reality—it is their money to begin with....

I would much rather allow them—the rich—to keep some of their money at home versus taking it overseas and not have benefit to it at all, if I was the government. "But trickle-down economics doesn't work!" Ah, the age-old argument to justify taking money from someone who didn't earn it and giving it to the masses. For starters, trickle-down economics isn't a real thing. What is real is when you have a business, have a product or services, employ people, and have customers who spend money at your establishment. That is called currency flow. It's an ecosystem within itself. The money from the customers supports and pays the business owner, covers the cost of goods and

14 US Congress, An Act to provide for reconciliation pursuant to titles II and V of the concurrent resolution on the budget for fiscal year 2018, Congress.gov, 2017, https://www.congress.gov/bill/115th-congress/house-bill/1/text.

services, supports employees, and helps the business keep its lights on. Those employees that are paid in turn support other businesses or the current business, and the cycle repeats itself. Other incidentals are investments, entertainment, and travel—with the additional disposable income. So, if we are to define trickle-down economics—that would be the short title for what I have explained.

From an individual standpoint, the tax cuts will tremendously help many people across the US. As someone once put it, "Half of America already doesn't pay taxes" [*I believe it was Dave Ramsey; not exactly sure*], which is true. Those unemployed, underemployed, and simply living off the welfare system aren't paying taxes—or much in taxes, if they are. In fact, these very people are getting paid. Those who are in the tax-paying part of society will see additional credits for children—doubling, in fact!

▪ CHAPTER 2 ▪

MAINSTREAM MEDIA AND SOCIAL MEDIA

LEFT-LEANING MEDIA

Throughout the presidency of Donald Trump, the media—particularly the left-leaning outlets—took a sharp nosedive in what we've collectively known as true journalism. There is historical evidence of the age-old practice of using sound bites and partial statements to paint a negative picture of a person, but during this particular administration, it seems as though it was much more prevalent than it had been with any other political figure. A couple of running sound bite–ladened narratives the media ran with included the hot-mic conversation between Billy Bush and Donald Trump, where he talked about being a star and having women around him that would allow him to do whatever he wanted—including grabbing them by the…well, you know by now.[15] The other one was about the Charlottesville protest, where a woman by the name of Heather Heyer was killed by one of the extremist protestors. I am not going to speculate who or what he was affiliated with, but the suspicion is enough to know that he was radicalized.

---

15 "BIAS ALERT: Did NBC sit on Trump hot mic footage?" Fox News, October 11, 2016, https://www.foxnews.com/politics/bias-alert-did-nbc-sit-on-trump-hot-mic-footage.

President Trump was accused of saying, "There were fine people on both sides."[16] The media portrayed him as including extremists and white supremacists. This was a blatant lie and false narrative that ran in the media for months, if not several years.

There are three things from the left stream media that one can easily identify in order to prepare themselves as to whether or not they (the audience) are about to receive actual news or opinions based on news: (1) The host/panel, (2) the network and time of day, and (3) the overemphasis of the "reporting," also known as aggrandizing the story. We see much of this with networks such as CNN, MSNBC, and even Fox News. According to CNN, Newsmax and OANN have come under fire in recent months because of their overtly biased reporting and gravitas towards the MAGA movement's 2020 election claims.[17] This, in my opinion, is fine because they let it be known up front. At this juncture of this writing, literally ten months have gone by. So much crap has happened that I don't even know where to begin. Since we're on the topic of media, Chris Cuomo of CNN, you know the guy—his brother was the governor of New York who resigned over sexual harassment scandals. Cuomo was fired from CNN for his involvement in his brother's ordeal, along with some other toxic, work-related issues.[18] *The View* is still on the air, unfortunately, despite the suspensions of Whoopi Goldberg and the repeated ignorant and ill-informed commentary by the other

---

16 "Read the complete transcript of President Trump's remarks at Trump Tower on Charlottesville," *Los Angeles Times,* August 15, 2017, https://www.latimes.com/politics/la-na-pol-trump-charlottesville-transcript-20170815-story.html.

17 . "Newsmax and OANN are telling lies about the election as more people tune in," CNN Business, 2020, https://www.cnn.com/videos/business/2020/11/23/newsmax-oan-trump-conspiracy-theories-ratings-orig-vf.cnnbusiness.

18 Julia Marsh, Dana Kennedy, and Mary Kay Linge, "Chris Cuomo fired from CNN over involvement with brother Andrew's scandals," *New York Post,* December 5, 2021, https://nypost.com/2021/12/04/chris-cuomo-fired-from-cnn-over-involvement-with-brother-andrews-scandals/.

cohosts, such as Sunny Hostin and Joy Behar. CNN went on to revamp their lineup and got rid of some more folks like Brian Stelter. I can honestly say I've never caught any of his shows, so I can't give an honest opinion, although his off-camera and guest appearances told me enough about him and what his show would be about. Also canceled from primetime was Don Lemon, though I am surprised he hasn't been outright fired at this point. Let's move over to MSNBC. Joy Reid still has a job—for now—although she's skating on very thin ice in her career. I honestly think they are only keeping her around because she has enough African American followers that her dismissal followed with an alleged "racism was the cause" attack would tank the network completely. So MSNBC is playing it smart and keeping her on board despite the repeated calls to get rid of her. **Update here: Joy Reid was finally fired on February 25, 2025.**[19] Rachel Maddow had a big enough meltdown that she left the network for a bit. Perhaps she will finally have a new look in her next endeavor. I was sick of seeing the same black blazer and blouse for the last five-years...[20]

The main[lame]stream media have been under so much fire and criticism that many of the millions of viewers have turned to alternative media outlets and podcasters in recent years. After all, these places still cover the news and whatever may be going on out there to your liking. The biggest difference is that the contemporary news media are not running an agenda—at least, not one that you can affect. Most of the contemporary media person-

---

19 Justin Baragona, "Joy Reid's final show: Fired MSNBC host leaves viewers with dire message after controversial axing," *The Independent*, February 25, 2025, https://www.the-independent.com/news/world/americas/us-politics/joy-reid-final-show-fascism-b2704385.html.

20 David Bauder, "Rachel Maddow returns to MSNBC, will switch to once a week," *Rocky Mountain Outlook*, April 11, 2022, https://www.rmoutlook.com/lifestyle/rachel-maddow-returns-to-msnbc-will-switch-to-once-a-week-5256313.

alities are trying to gain enough followers to get their channels or their brand monetized. Your role in all of this? Like, subscribe, hit the notification bell, and share. Pretty simple stuff. The tide that finally turned viewers away from the mainstream media was the suppression of the Hunter Biden laptop story that was released by the *New York Post* but suppressed by Twitter (now known as X) and Facebook.[21] [22] The media wouldn't talk about it or dismissed it as Russian disinformation. All of this in an effort to keep voters from being swayed by Joe Biden's alleged business dealings and alleged selling of his name and position as vice president through Hunter's shady and illegal businesses and practices. You are probably wondering how we still ended up with a Biden administration and Hunter is still walking around scot-free like he's society's role model of a son? Well, it's simple—the mainstream media has not expressed outrage—why should you?

In September of 2022, I rebranded my internet-based television show, *The NEW with Randy & April* to *Purham & Associates.* It streams live on TECN.TV as well as my Twitter and Facebook pages. The rebrand happened for a couple of reasons. First, my now estranged and soon-to-be ex-wife [*Officially divorced as of December of 2024*] didn't want to have anything to do with me and what I/we were discussing on my shows—especially around hardcore conservative politics. She got phone calls and text messages from her liberal friends lambasting her for associating with a vile and disgusting person such as me, so she felt she needed to

21 The Editors, "Biden's Social-Media Censorship Regime," *National Review,* August 28, 2024, https://www.nationalreview.com/2024/08/bidens-social-media-censorship-regime/.

22 House Judiciary Committee Press Release, "Testimony Reveals FBI Employees Who Warned Social Media Companies about Hack and Leak Operation Knew Hunter Biden Laptop Wasn't Russian Disinformation," July 20, 2023, https://judiciary.house.gov/media/press-releases/testimony-reveals-fbi-employees-who-warned-social-media-companies-about-hack.

distance herself from me "publicly." The second reason is that the direction my show was taking encompassed having more guests from all walks of life discussing the run-of-the-mill topics of the week. I enjoy this format better than me and, sometimes, her and me, discussing the headlines of the week. I say all that to highlight one important point. It is okay to recognize when change and something new needs to happen in the media. The legacy media outlets have not figured that out yet and are crashing and burning one pundit at a time. Perhaps *Morning Joe*'s Joe Scarborough and Mika Brzezinski should take some notes!

RIGHT-LEANING MEDIA

Much of the mainstream media consists of left-wing personalities that will not really engage in civil and meaningful conversation with those on the right. It almost seems that this is by genetic default. However, right-wing media outlets—notably Fox News—took a shellacking since 2020's election night for cosigning on calling Arizona prematurely for Joe Biden.[23] [24] Since then, Fox's ratings have taken a nosedive with conservative viewers although they still outpaced the other networks. This paradigm shift gave rise to MAGA-based media outlets like Real America's Voice and Right Side Broadcasting Network. While these networks have not gone corporate in nature yet, the corporate world—particularly Disney—will dangle a big enough check in front of them to make them fold. Networks like TECN will not give in to such pressures because of the organizational structure of independent hosts that

---

23 David Bauder, "Two Fox News political executives out after Arizona call," Associated Press, January 19, 2021, https://apnews.com/article/joe-biden-donald-trump-arizona-elections-a11f8112a58eb45854be59f64d47e1dc.

24 Election Night Channel, "When Fox News called Arizona for Joe Biden (Election 2020)," YouTube, November 8, 2020, https://www.youtube.com/watch?v=wrDYcS9qskE.

are in full control of their own content and their shows. If they choose to go to a larger network or venture into something different, that is their choice. NTD and Epoch Times are also growing in viewership and followers for their down-the-middle journalism. I will be a bit partial here and say that my favorite show with NTD is *China in Focus* with Tiffany Meier.

Some notables on the right have been shuffled around as well. Chris Wallace from Fox left to go over to CNN to help launch their now-defunct CNN+ platform. He grew disgusted with Fox's direction of being pro-MAGA along with the guests who were strong Trump supporters. Tomi Lahren was essentially dismissed from Fox News but does make some commentary-based appearances on occasion. She went on to host her own show with BlazeTV, a growing, right-leaning network. Hosts like Glenn Beck and Mark Levin continue to trailblaze with their content. I presently can't think of any other right-leaning up-and-coming networks, so if I missed you, it was not an intentional slight. OAN was under fire earlier in the year by leftists who called for DirectTV (AT&T) to cancel their contract, thus essentially deplatforming them. Of course, DirectTV gave in to the woke mob and terminated their contract.[25] More on woke and cancel culture later. This particular action had me pretty upset. Since when was it okay for a certain segment of the population to demand what programs carriers should carry? I subsequently canceled my AT&T direct stream service after this and a few other things I did not agree with by AT&T. Unfortunately, I cannot cancel my cell phone service until the contract term ends.

25 Lexi Lonas Cochran, "DirecTV declines to renew OAN contract," *The Hill*, January 14, 2022, https://thehill.com/homenews/media/589871-directv-declines-to-renew-one-america-news-networks-contract/.

Whatever source of media you use to get your information, try and approach it with the understanding and knowledge that it got its source from somewhere else. Depending on the leaning of that source, your main source may not bring you all the information or even the facts for that matter. Sensationalizing the news has become the thing to do, and it is often the only way these media outlets will bring it to you over the airwaves—because they are paid to do it that way.

SOCIAL MEDIA INFLUENCERS (SMI)

Aside from your television-based media personalities, you have thousands if not hundreds of thousands of social media influencers ranging from everything you can literally think of—and they are the "expert" at whatever that thing is. This is perfectly fine in a world of interconnectivity and curiosity. Recommendations to click, like, and subscribe is how they get paid—usually—and they've become a trend or hashtag of some sort for more views and followers. Get really creative, and they become "viral." Being a SMI has its ups and downs. The upside is you get to become famous for whatever it is that you do, and you can make a lot of money from it and even get a lot of free stuff from companies that choose to advertise and sponsor you. Some even have the luck of getting corporate sponsorships.

The downside—if you can really call it that—is that you have literally hundreds of thousands if not millions of people prying into every waking and sleeping moment of your life. They expect you to respond to their comments, emails, and they definitely want you to shout out their names so they can become famous or an influencer too. These pressures can be too much for anyone, let alone a barely budding teenager or young adult who hasn't figured out how to do their taxes yet. But somehow, they are relied upon to give expert advice on certain things—around the clock! The previously mentioned legacy media, corporations, and our lovely elected officials have mastered the art of taking advantage of these unexpecting gurus and leverage their influencing powers to deliver their agenda—for a nominal fee of course.

During the FTX bitcoin exchange downfall in late 2022, many celebrities came under fire and under investigation for their advocacy and marketing of FTX along with other companies that went bust virtually overnight.[26] Many influencers advocated for people to take the COVID-19 vaccines to help the pharmaceutical companies combat the hesitancy of the population at large, knowing full well that they themselves had slapped on a Band-Aid, taken the check, and never actually took the vaccine but got fake shot records or vaccine cards.[27] CRIMINAL. So the next time your favorite influencer or celebrity of sorts pushes some commercial for something, you should challenge them—in fact, mandate—that they use the product on a live stream at the prescribed/recommended usage to convince you that they are not only the spokesperson, but they are truly also a customer or client.

26 Yvette Brend, "Celebs like Tom Brady, Larry David did ads for crypto giant FTX. Now they're getting sued," CBC, November 19, 2022, https://www.cbc.ca/news/business/bankruptcy-class-action-ftx-cryptocurrency-bailout-bankman-fried-1.6655836.

27 Lioness of Judah Ministry, "Safe and Effective: 2,000 Hollywood Celebrities, European Elite Caught with Fake Vaccination Passports," *Exposing the Darkness*, January 14, 2025, https://lionessofjudah.substack.com/p/safe-and-effective-2000-hollywood?utm_campaign=post&utm_medium=web.

▪ CHAPTER 3 ▪

INDOCTRINATION OF THE AMERICAN PEOPLE

THE SUMMER OF LOVE

I'll take you back to the summer of 2020, the summer of love with the riots surrounding the death of George Floyd. While tragic, it is actually nothing new in the world, let alone in America. The manner in which he died was egregious, and the sentencing the former cops got for their role and involvement is justified—no one can argue against it. However, the media—see the previous chapter—took no issue with sensationalizing the incident and stoked the flames of already emotionally triggered Americans across the country, which in turn erupted American cities across the country into chaos. Black Lives Matter (BLM) and Antifa emerged prominently in everything surrounding the Floyd death and the riots. They used a beautifully crafted narrative that garnered the support of millions from around the world that Black lives mattered and that it was time for change. White liberals jumped on board and fomented the opportunity to be the proverbial savior to Black people by initiating their own agenda with their own militant wing known as Antifa.

Antifa encouraged and engaged in riots in cities where there was a strong Black population—cities such as Atlanta, Chicago, Austin, Minneapolis, Seattle, Phoenix, and Baltimore.[28] Blacks who are generally conservative in nature immediately took notice at who the players were in these riots: young white liberals and young impressionable Blacks, who were told they were oppressed and the rioting and looting was a form of reparation by those young white liberals. When Blacks took to the media to call out what was happening, BLM immediately attacked them for being race traitors, not supporting the cause, and other guilt-shaming tactics to silence nonconforming Blacks and others who were not supportive of the rioting and general violence that took place. BLM and Antifa were so convincing that they got elected officials to buy into their agenda/narrative. Parts of Seattle were under siege with the blocking off of certain areas, and their mayor thought it was cool.[29] Detroit and Minneapolis pulled these same antics, and as the crime and assaults skyrocketed in these areas, the National Guard and local police were finally given the green light to bust these places up.

I'll spare further details about BLM's and Antifa's actions during 2020. BLM cofounder Patrisse Cullors subsequently came under fire for buying mansions and giving family members large sums of money, and other chapter leaders woke up to the sham when they asked for funding to rebuild their communities—that they

---

28 Massod Farivar, "Anarchist Groups Tied to Riots in 4 US Cities," Voice of America, September 16, 2020, https://www.voanews.com/a/extremism-watch_anarchist-groups-tied-riots-4-us-cities/6195936.html.

29 Michael Brown, "The mayor of Seattle has a rude awakening about CHOP," *The Christian Post,* July 2, 2020, https://www.christianpost.com/voices/the-mayor-of-seattle-has-a-rude-awakening-about-chop.html.

destroyed but got nothing for it during the riots.[30] [31] Ironically, people still run around chanting "Black Lives Matter," not because they believe that Black lives actually matter, but because they still believe in the agenda—because they are still brainwashed despite the evidence and information presented to them. Antifa is still very much active; they have taken to social media to troll and have canceled anyone they disagree with, along with their messages. Dressed in all black, with ski-masks and backpacks full of Soros-funded goodies, these pipsqueaks gather in large crowds, often near a Starbucks, to wreak mayhem on unsuspecting communities, patrons, or citizens out minding their business. In California, an Antifa protest erupted, and presumably members of Proud Boys intercepted this group, dousing them with bear spray.[32] The cops that were on scene turned a blind eye, but we'll say they were overwhelmed and called it good.

CRT AND SEL

Critical Race Theory

In the early part of 2021, the latest craze that hit the social scene was pushing this thing called critical race theory (CRT) and social-emotional learning (SEL) in our public school systems. The left immediately defended CRT as being *true history*! and *telling historical events as they actually happened*—as if they were actually there to witness it themselves. CRT is derived from Karl Marx's

30 Isabel Vincent, "BLM spent at least $12M on luxury properties in LA, Toronto: tax filing," *New York Post,* May 19, 2022, https://nypost.com/2022/05/17/black-lives-matter-spent-at-least-12-million-on-mansions/.

31 Julian Baron, "Black Lives Matter faces growing rift with local chapters over finances and transparency," Fox45News, December 3, 2020, https://foxbaltimore.com/news/nation-world/black-lives-matter-faces-rift-with-local-chapters-over-finances.

32 ABC 7 News Bay Area, "Trump Rally turns violent in Sacramento as Proud Boys, Antifa face off," YouTube, November 15, 2020, https://www.youtube.com/watch?v=I7yHxW6eIqI.

theory, commonly known as Marxism, which revolves around the conflict between the bourgeoisie and the proletariat.[33] In this rendition, it is the oppressed and the oppressors, where, if you are white, you are the oppressor, and if you are any kind of person of the minority bloc, you are automatically the oppressed, despite the amount of success that you have personally achieved.[34] To this very day in October of 2022, I have actually yet to meet anyone in person who actually subscribes to this nonsense—but here we are talking about it.

Defenders of CRT also tried to push the idea that it was only being taught in college law classes at only certain schools. As it turns out, not only was it being pushed and taught in K-12 schools, but the curriculum was designed to be age- and grade-appropriate for the students. This was discovered through the proactive involvement of parents across the country, who sounded the alarm. This eventually resulted in the National School Boards Association (NSBA) writing to the Department of Justice to go after parents and label them as "domestic terrorists" for attending and expressing their concerns at public school board meetings.[35] The nationwide blowback was vociferous to say the least. The leaked memo from the NSBA sparked so much outrage that many members of the NSBA canceled their memberships, and school boards across the country withdrew their association from the

---

33 Walter Myers III, "Critical Race Theory—The Marxist Trojan Horse," Discovery Institute, August 5, 2021, https://www.discovery.org/education/2021/08/05/critical-race-theory-the-marxist-trojan-horse/.

34 Neal Hardin, "What Is Critical Race Theory?" Alliance Defending Freedom, October 4, 2021, https://adflegal.org/article/what-critical-race-theory/.

35 Defending Education Press Release, "Full NSBA Letter to Biden Administration and Department of Justice Memo," November 29, 2021, https://defendinged.org/press-releases/full-nsba-letter-to-biden-administration-and-department-of-justice-memo/.

national level as well.[36] Subsequently, the Biden administration initially doubled down on the incendiary comments made in the letter, but ultimately retracted those statements—as did the NSBA by issuing an apology letter. Nonetheless, the damage was done and the DOJ still continued to harass parents who made their voices heard at school board meetings concerning CRT.

In 2019, Nikole Hannah-Jones, a relatively unknown journalist at the time, published an article titled "The 1619 Project" in *The New York Times Magazine*. This hit piece on history alleged that the nation's founding was actually in 1619, when the first set of slaves arrived in the colonies, and not in 1776, when the nation declared its independence from Britain.[37] This article created much stir and essentially gave birth to the revisionary agenda of the CRT. Historians from all sectors of academia denounced and even wrote books to counter the article. A couple of years later, Hannah-Jones was denied tenure at the University of North Carolina at Chapel Hill, but later reached a settlement over disputes with her contract.[38] [39] There was a lot of mess surrounding her debacle with UNC, but I won't get into it here; the point I'm making is that you had a journalist who was rewriting history,

---

36 Jeff Johnston, "State School Board Associations Separating from National School Boards Association," Daily Citizen, December 10, 2021, https://dailycitizen.focusonthefamily.com/state-school-board-associations-separating-from-national-school-boards-association/.

37 The 1619 Project—Interactive, *New York Times Magazine,* September 4, 2019, https://www.nytimes.com/interactive/2019/08/14/magazine/1619-america-slavery.html.

38 "Nikole Hannah-Jones Issues Statement on Decision to Decline Tenure Offer at University of North Carolina-Chapel Hill and to Accept Knight Chair Appointment at Howard University," Legal Defense Fund, July 6, 2021, https://www.naacpldf.org/press-release/nikole-hannah-jones-issues-statement-on-decision-to-decline-tenure-offer-at-university-of-north-carolina-chapel-hill-and-to-accept-knight-chair-appointment-at-howard-university/.

39 "Nikole Hannah-Jones Reaches Settlement Agreement with the University of North Carolina at Chapel Hill," Legal Defense Fund, July 16, 2022, https://www.naacpldf.org/press-release/nikole-hannah-jones-reaches-settlement-agreement-with-the-university-of-north-carolina-at-chapel-hill/.

and people accepted it as facts, paid her as a credible voice, and allowed her to spread this information as facts, despite the actual historical artifacts and centuries of literal documentation of what transpired from 16-whenever onward. But anyways...

SEL—Social-Emotional Learning

I've yet to receive a satisfying answer as to how SEL will prepare our posterity for competition in the real world, let alone getting through the everyday rigors of life without self-imploding into emotional breakdowns at the sign of a stressful moment. But this is where we are in the world now. We have substituted arithmetic, history, science, reading, English literature, and most importantly, in my opinion, social studies—all for lessons on activism, sensitivity to others' feelings, how to satisfy genitals, and what books and movies we will cancel before next semester starts. These are all the things OUR children are now being subjugated to in the public education domain—regardless of grade and type of educational institution.

Proponents of SEL will tell you that it is important for children to learn the emotional triggers and causal factors to the social behaviors surrounding their environment. The Collaborative for Academic, Social, and Emotional Learning (CASEL) website offers a more glowing definition of SEL:

> Social-emotional learning (SEL) is the process of developing the self-awareness, self-control, and interpersonal skills that are vital for school, work, and life success. People with strong social-emotional skills are better able to cope with everyday challenges and benefit academically, professionally, and socially. From effective problem-solving to self-discipline, from impulse control to

emotion management and more, SEL provides a foundation for positive, long-term effects on kids, adults, and communities.[40]

Don't get me wrong here; I am by no means saying that children—or even adults—should not get the developmental skills necessary to be able to adequately function in society; however, I am saying it should not be the central theme in the academic arena. Now, we see the direct and immediate results of children being triggered by various things that were normalized for folks who grew up in the US. As a side note, I had a conversation with one of my daughters, and she expressed in her "infinite wisdom" that people of my generation are screwed up and that our parenting methods screwed up the subsequent generations because they are not able to cope with the environment of today because WE did not prepare them for it. Interesting, huh? That was my summation of the conversation. I literally had no words to respond to that nonsense.

I fully recognize that our generation—those born between the 1970s through the 1990s—is much different than the generation of today. We didn't have social media—not like that—we were forced to go outside on the weekends right after Saturday morning cartoons and were mandated to stay outside until the streetlights came on. The fights, the drive-by shootings, the crackheads and prostitutes were our "street teachers." It was reminiscent of the movie *Rocky IV* when Ivan Drago said, "If he dies, he dies...."[41] This is often what we thought our parents thought about us when

40 "What Is the CASEL Framework?" CASEL, 2023, https://casel.org/fundamentals-of-sel/what-is-the-casel-framework/#:~:text=Self%2Dawareness:%20The%20abilities%20to,sense%20of%20confidence%20and%20purpose.

41 joe mclemore, "Ivan Drago - If he dies, he dies," YouTube, March 3, 2016, https://www.youtube.com/watch?v=WvAeWtyZ-uE.

they kicked us out the house for the day. We adapted and overcame our obstacles, bullets, fists, and broken bottles. And oh, by the way, you're not going to keep running in and out of the house for water; drink from the spicket on the side of the house or somebody's house or the fire hydrant if it was busted open during the summer. And you better not come walking in the house more than five minutes after the streetlights came on. This literally was our social-emotional learning.

I am glad to see there are parents out there today in 2023 that are adopting this model of raising children (*not the SEL stuff, but the old-school model*). Let the children play! Let them learn how to navigate those social challenges on their own. Sure, have a watchful eye for life-threatening hazards, but keep a distance and stop coddling these kids. Don't be helicopter parents, but don't be neglectful or naive parents, either. There was a study done out in Finland where they observed children during recess playing, fighting, and doing what kids do. At the end of the study, it was determined that such children are more than well-suited to sort out their issues versus kids who had adults watching over them and mediating every dispute or intervening at the moment of a fall off the merry-go-round.[42] Children will grow up and thank you later—or hate you later—for allowing them to be who they were meant to be. As a proponent of Darwinism, let the strongest survive!

42 Jon Henley et al., "'Let children play': the educational message from across Europe," *The Guardian,* April 23, 2021, https://www.theguardian.com/society/2021/apr/23/let-children-play-the-educational-message-from-across-europe.

▪ CHAPTER 4 ▪

HISTORY AND HIS-STORY

WHO LIVES, WHO DIES, WHO TELLS YOUR STORY?

I attribute the subtitle of this chapter to the title of a song from the play *Hamilton.* It is fitting because there is an old adage that goes, "Those who win the war tell the story (or write the history)." Both of these sayings are very true. Which brings me to the next point. History, as we know it, is composed of tales of times of old passed down through storytelling, documents, and summaries of events packaged into a narrative that is suitable for the audience receiving it. Whether that is the story about the fall of Rome, the Ottoman Empire, how slavery was—wherever it happened, the American Revolution, the Civil War, or even the Persian Gulf War. All of these events entailed people, their personal stories, or events within them and around them—and someone had to tell those stories, whether it was them or someone else much, much later.

While history in itself may be highly accurate, the finite details may not be so. After all, there are gaps in every story, and those gaps need to be filled. This goes back to another adage, "Your side, their side, and what really happened." This is why, in our society today, history as we once knew it has become very uncomfortable to discuss. This essentially is how "cancel culture" was born.

People came across materials that THEY found to be offensive and complained about it and advocated to have it erased as if it never happened. Never to be discussed again, never published, never produced, never to be spoken of—CANCELED. This is also where revisionism of history comes into play. Creative writing like "The 1619 Project" is a stark example of revisionist history getting pawned off as the truth, the whole truth, and nothing but the truth. When technically, it was not so to any degree.

History, no matter how uncomfortable or shameful it was, is just that—history! We learn from it, accept it, grow from it, and become or do better from it. "When you know better, you do better" is what I heard often growing up. But seemingly, we are in an age where when we know better, we want to punish the past for not being better. A generation from now, we will find members of society repeating things that the current generation grew away from because no one taught them that it was not cool to do or say those things. Why? Because we canceled the history that taught us better. Can you imagine if the Bible was canceled? How about if *Barney & Friends* or *Sesame Street* got canceled? Remember your favorite TV show growing up as a teenager that you watched or passively listened to in the background as you got ready for school, just to ditch it later? CANCELED! Classic novels like *To Kill a Mockingbird* and Agatha Christie's mysteries are now subject to cancellation because they offended someone. Learning about Ruby Bridges and the civil rights movement during a course for Black History Month was canceled—the class was literally stopped—because someone was offended.[43] YOU CAN'T MAKE THIS STUFF UP!

---

43 Gary C. Harrell, "Ruby Bridges, Cancel Culture & the Denial of American History," Medium, February 9, 2022, https://gcharrell1975.medium.com/ruby-bridges-cancel-culture-the-denial-of-american-history-a0ccc3d0902b.

The Civil War was a very dark time in our country's young history. The North versus the South, brother against brother, state against state. All over taxation and slavery—largely slavery, but taxation also played a part. There are many historical events surrounding what happened during the Civil War and slavery in those years. Slaves fought on both sides—but that is rarely discussed. Slave owners freed their slaves out of guilt because of the war—that, too, is rarely discussed. Confederate generals and soldiers largely didn't even own a slave—that is rarely discussed. But what is discussed is the fact that there are monuments and military bases named after or "honoring" the confederate southern fighters. But why? No one ever asks that question. No one cares. The South lost and they should not be honored or remembered, PERIOD! Well, how will future generations know who these folks were, what they looked like, what they did? These and them are integral parts of the WHOLE story. PUT THEM IN A MUSEUM! They will say, well, how many people really go to museums versus walking through a random park and seeing a statue with a little blurb about it? The point of it all is that cancel culture is utterly stupid, and it is manifesting self-implosion as we speak.

While I lived in Frederick, Maryland—actually stationed there in the Army—I had the opportunity to visit many Civil War battlefields, from Gettysburg and Monocacy to Harpers Ferry and Manassas. Walking and running up and down the trails and hills of the land that once was traversed by men who fought to keep my ancestors in chains and to set them free was something remarkable. Reading the plaques, the inscriptions, and other explainers both inside museums and out on these battlefields is something most people that visit these places rarely do. They just walk through, snap a few pictures, and keep it moving. But rarely do we ever take the time to immerse ourselves in the moment of history.

HIS-STORY

The African American experience in the United States is very, very unique. Since the 1960s, African Americans have registered at 13 percent of the US population, while nearly every other minority group has grown. Many factors affect the reasons why: high murder rates, high incarceration, high infant mortality rates, high rates of diseases and medical issues, high abortion rates—and, of course, there is always slavery. Yes, you read that right. Slavery is a factor in the low population rate among African Americans in the United States because of causal factors throughout history. Slavery played a pivotal role in the steady decrease in the childbearing rate over the decades. It was commonplace during slavery and before—back in Africa—for parents to have numerous children, like in the teens or high single digits. Most families of the eighteenth century were like this—regardless of color. The decline in childbearing among African Americans began for most families in the 1950s, as Jim Crow and the civil rights movement shifted the focus onto survival so that there would be as few to take care of as possible in the event movement in a hasty fashion was necessary.

In the urban population centers or highly concentrated Black communities, you will find a few families with large numbers of children because it simply pays. Government welfare programs such as WIC, SNAP, or EBT (food stamps) benefit large single-parent homes financially, thus creating this stigma within the Black community of "welfare queens." I am personally a by-product of this system and thoroughly understand how it works. Black men are discouraged from being in the home and co-parenting because it actually financially penalizes families where low-wage jobs in the community is a huge factor for large families. These very men—most of them—find themselves struggling to earn an honest living and perpetuate a pattern of having children out of wedlock with multiple women. While this destructive behavior may seem gratifying to the grand scheme of population growth, it led to other nefarious means of income production such as drug selling, stealing, and robbing, all of which are by-products of murder in most cases in the Black community, and subsequently lead to prolonged prison sentences.

Because Blacks are not victors in this war on Black America, they don't get to tell the story of how these social ills affect their livelihoods. Rather, people—especially of other ethnicities—tell their story from their perspective and that is what is published, produced, and accepted among society in general. You may have thought: "What is this 'war' on Black America, and who is waging it?" Democrats! Duh! It goes without real research that the Democratic Party controls ALL the urban population centers of Blacks and minorities in the United States. This is just based on simple math, common sense, and watching CNN and MSNBC. As a matter of fact, just drive through a Black community and observe. The plight of Black America isn't because Black Americans don't want better or can't do better; it's because they are not ALLOWED to do better. It has been embedded into the minds of Blacks that when you try to become educated, want prosperity for you and your family, or think for yourself, you are an "Uncle Tom," a "coon," or some other racial epithet of the day because you are not toeing the party line and ideology.[44]

This mindset and run-of-the-mill trap has encapsulated Black America for decades and has become the accepting factor among every other racial group in America, every political party, and

44 Paul Bond, "Meet the Young, Black Conservatives Who Are Stumping for Trump—Despite the Backlash," *Newsweek,* October 15, 2020, https://www.newsweek.com/meet-young-black-conservatives-who-are-stumping-trumpdespite-backlash-1538815.

every economic and political ecosystem around the world. Where is the lie in the thought that when a Black person enters the room, people—no matter what their color is—will automatically assume that Black person is politically aligned with the Democratic Party? Why is this? The conversation is taboo among ALL other minority groups. But for Black America, you are a Democrat or a foe.[45] There has been some conditioning somewhere between the end of the Civil War and the Great Society that implanted this ideological scheme. I have not been able to quite pinpoint it, but it is very disturbing, nonetheless, considering that WE are literally the only minority bloc in America that is the topic of conversation for voting for candidates in certain districts and certain elections.

Newsflash. This just in. Hispanics are now the largest minority bloc in America, and Blacks are not considered a political force anymore! Just when Black America thought they had some political leverage in the twenty-first century, it was snatched right from underneath them like it was standard protocol. President Joseph R. Biden and company's (Democrat's) "open border policy" ushered in a new generation and population of voters—and they are not Black. In fact, they are mostly from South American countries, with only a few thousand from the Caribbean and African countries. This very action alone ballooned the American Hispanic population to a whopping 19 percent[46]—that we can actually account for—not to mention the push for mail-in voting, ID-less in-person voting, and a host of other at-will voting measures that will diminish the voting power of Black America for

45 Shelby Steele, "The Loneliness of the "Black Conservative," Hoover Institution, January 30, 1999, https://www.hoover.org/research/loneliness-black-conservative.

46 Luisa N Borrell and Anahi Viladrich, "The Hispanic/Latino Population in the United States: Our Black Identity, Our Health and Well-Being," National Library of Medicine, Am J Public Health, DOI: 10.2105/AJPH.2024.307682, July 2024, https://pmc.ncbi.nlm.nih.gov/articles/PMC11292280/#:~:text=The%20Hispanic/Latino%20population%20represents,by%202050%20(128%20million).

eternity. With the evidence plain and clear and the verdict already rendered, there are dedicated—or as I say, complicit—Black Americans that still ride the Democratic Tammany Hall machine regardless of the peril it may impose. It's simply amazing to see.

Black America will never get to tell their story the way they want to or the way it needs to be told. They did not win the war. They did not engage in the battles hard enough, there was too much division among the ranks, and they certainly don't have the numbers for an all-out assault in the near or distant future. WE are doomed to accept the status quo and get in where we fit in. Concessions were given, deals were made, and Black America sold itself out for the idea and the appearance that something was being accomplished. The evidence is clear—don't take my word for it. Black America was duped into believing that progress was made. "Allegedly," President Lyndon B. Johnson was quoted thus:

> These Negroes, they're getting pretty uppity these days and that's a problem for us since they've got something now they never had before, the political pull to back up their uppityness. Now we've got to do something about this, we've got to give them a little something, just enough to quiet them down, not enough to make a difference. For if we don't move at all, then their allies will line up against us and there'll be no way of stopping them, we'll lose the filibuster and there'll be no way of putting a brake on all sorts of wild legislation. It'll be Reconstruction all over again. [Said to Senator Richard Russell Jr. (D-GA) regarding the Civil Rights Act of 1957][47] [48]

47 Jon Miltimore, "Did LBJ Say, 'I'll have those n*ggers voting Democratic for 200 years'?" Intellectual Takeout, October 10, 2016, https://intellectualtakeout.org/2016/10/did-lbj-say-ill-have-those-nggers-voting-democratic-for-200-years/.

48 "Lyndon B. Johnson, Quotes, Quotable Quotes," Goodreads, 2025, https://www.goodreads.com/quotes/7107768-these-negroes-they-re-getting-pretty-uppity-these-days-and-that-s.

While chanting "Black Lives Matter" and preaching for diversity, equity, and inclusion, all looks great and sounds good. The reality is that these hopes and dreams will be, and can be, crushed without a bat of an eye—if greater America so decrees. This is HISTORY, not HIS-STORY.

▪ CHAPTER 5 ▪

NO LIVES MATTER

HYPOCRISY MATTERS

When George Floyd was killed by Minneapolis police officers in the summer of 2020, the mantra of the BLM organization—"Black lives matter!"—became the rallying cry for both racial and social justice, not only in America but around the world. For some odd reason, the very idea that a Black person's life mattering has to be spoken aloud and become a political issue still baffles me. Chanting "Black lives matter!" became politicized when it was met with "All lives matter!" This chant became the pushback from the political neutral zone, meaning it came from both sides of the aisle, but it was streaming largely and typically from suburban whites who wanted to express the idea that all lives mattered and not just Blacks, as perceived to be implied.[49] This new mantra further pissed off the political (*Black*) left, and then "All lives matter!" became a racist statement. I kid you not! Black lives do matter. So do all lives for that matter; however, let's put both statements into context and reality.

During the protests, during the riots, during the policy proposals and advocacy of new legislation to address police brutality,

49 Participedia, "All Lives Matter," 2014, https://participedia.net/case/5563?lang=en.

numerous Blacks were murdered. The crimes that were committed resulted in little to no incarceration and destroyed communities and businesses. The grifting from the donors and sympathizers of the movement resulted in further distrust and sowed discontentment among members of the national and state chapters. All of these things spurned African Americans from all walks of life to rally behind the movement for one simple reason—it said Black lives matter. If you were a Black person and didn't ascribe to this idea, then you were immediately castigated as some kind of "Uncle Tom" or "bootlicker." Dare you to say "All lives matter!" you were surely to be socially lynched—lynched as in ridiculed through social media, and maybe literally too, depending on where you were located. White liberals immediately jumped on the bandwagon as they saw this as a great virtue-signaling opportunity to show the Black community that they are not inherently racists and that they understood and sympathized with their plights, solidifying their position as "allies" to the cause and willfully took a backseat—literally—during protests and events as they were told that Black voices needed to be heard, not white ones.[50 51]

This sentiment did not stop some white liberals from still grifting off the movement. Author, public speaker, and educationalist—*I suppose*—Robin DiAngelo wrote a book called *White Fragility,* which encouraged white people to stop being sensitive about what was going on and be more empathetic to Blacks and minorities. She later followed up with a webinar for Coca-

50 Maya Rosenberg, "White people need to be listening to black activists, not talking over them," *The Diamondback,* June 6, 2020, https://dbknews.com/2020/06/06/george-floyd-protests-racism-black-lives-matter/.

51 Chris Crass, "For White Anti-Racists Holding Back From Stepping Up in These Black Lives Matter Movement Times," Truthout, May 8, 2015, https://truthout.org/articles/for-white-anti-racists-holding-back-from-stepping-up-in-these-black-lives-matter-movement-times/.

Cola telling their employees "to try and be less white!"[52] Robin DiAngelo achieved instant success and fame from fellow liberals of all races for advocating for minorities in this fashion. She was also on a Zoom call, where she suggested that "People of Color should get away from white people and have a community of their own."[53] You can blink and think back to the Jim Crow South leading up to and during the civil rights era and reimagine when white Americans told Black citizens to get out of their neighborhoods and get their own communities. Liberals of today have a lot of echoing sentiments from the Democrat factions of the 1960s—before the alleged "switch." They just say things in a nicer way and make them sound endearing. I guess that is also why she titled one of her books *Nice Racism*—some Democrats have this knack for code-switching, ya know?

Patrisse Cullors, cofounder of the international BLM organization, rose to fame during the "summer of love," making appearances on all the media circuits and advocating the various positions and policies that needed to take place in the wake of the George Floyd killing. A devout, trained Marxist, she incorporated the teachings of Karl Marx and community organizer Saul Alinsky. The BLM movement raked in hundreds of millions of dollars worldwide and garnered support and endorsements from nearly every corporate organization in the world. However, in 2021, chapters such as the one in New York made a public outcry

52 Jake Bremner, "Coca-Cola faces backlash over seminar asking staff to 'be less white'," *The Independent,* February 24, 2021, https://www.the-independent.com/life-style/coca-cola-racism-robin-diangelo-coke-b1806122.html.

53 Ari Blaff, "Robin DiAngelo Advises People of Color to 'Get Away from White People'," *National Review,* March 21, 2023, https://www.yahoo.com/news/robin-diangelo-advises-people-color-195511417.html?guccounter=1&guce_referrer=aHR0cHM6Ly93d3cuZ29vZ2xlLmNvbS8&guce_referrer_sig=AQAAANOYomANOeLaLbpWvTD8y0fYOg3b8q1oWuFM77A7ATOVoe5snkQvSLtBb-cVHg0b8tw1ktmVDI8LOxK0wU8h-bzuOmsz0U93hzMXThpS8SIjUzC60cSWeorg8Wco1ojTrhFN3dUA-nTKSM4PQgOeMlViKOWKk4qy-6p6_bA99fbi.

over not receiving any money to fund their activities, and subsequently, sister organizations called out the parent company for its lavish spending and lack of financial transparency.[54] [55] Many chapter leaders saw the organization for what it really was when it was exposed that Cullors and her inner circle of cohorts, Alicia Garza and Opal Tometi, bought lavish mansions and other sorts of property in gated communities in California and other places like New York, Georgia, and the Bahamas.[56]

By 2022, the BLM movement came to an utter standstill. Exposed for the hypocrisy and grifting, the organization's founders seemingly disappeared into their lavish mansions to be never heard from since. Oddly enough, there are remnants that are still followers and advocates for BLM. Every time there is a death of a Black person at the hands of a white person who happens to be a cop, they pop up out of the woodwork. However, when there is "Black on Black" violence, they are nowhere to be found. Their excuse? That is not our cause! But Black lives matter, right? One would naturally think with a slogan such as "Black lives matter," it doesn't matter what the relating cause is, but rather that advocating for the preservation of BLACK LIVES is the central theme, whether that be through denouncing violence against Blacks, championing medical advancements and solutions for the most prevalent diseases in Black people—diabetes and heart disease—or simply changing the cultural aspects that contribute to the degenerative behaviors associated with Black depopulation.

54 Glen Ford, "BLM Chapters Demand 'Accountability' from Trio that Cashed in on the Movement," Black Agenda Report, December 3, 2020, https://www.blackagendareport.com/blm-chapters-demand-accountability-trio-cashed-movement.

55 Andrew Court and Harriet Alexander, "'How much of her money is actually going to charitable causes?' Head of NYC BLM chapter calls for probe into organization's co-founder as it's revealed 'she has spent $3MILLION on FOUR luxury homes'," Daily Mail, April 11, 2021, https://www.dailymail.co.uk/news/article-9458259/Head-NYCs-BLM-chapter-calls-probe-founder-purchased-expensive-homes.html.

56 Court and Alexander, "How much of her money..."

But instead, they remember "Black lives matter" only when they are the "victim" of White cops.

ALL LIVES MATTER

From 2019 through 2020, the chants of "Black lives matter" in the streets of YOU NAME IT CITY were often met with chants of "All lives matter!" Whether this was to say that not just Black lives mattered, but all lives truly mattered, or if it was a dog whistle to say that all lives mattered except Black ones, it made for interesting discussions as to how the Left turned "All lives matter!" into a solely white supremacist statement when in fact many minorities thought the sentiment was more unifying than divisive. I don't know how "All lives matter" became the rally cry for the Right and not everyone. And I don't know how one could extrapolate that to imply that it diminished the value of Black lives. "All" should be inclusive or include everyone or everything—am I off here?

If you are a Black person and you came face-to-face with a BLM activist and you said within the content of a conversation, "Well, all lives matter..." you would be met with such hatred and vitriol that your head would spin. You'd be immediately labeled as a white-supremacist boot-licking coon, and any other associated expletive or adjective that is used to denigrate you for your belief system that, well, every life matters. Never mind the religious ones who truly believe that all lives do matter and that Jesus died for us all and our sins collectively. The approach to that is immediately dismissed as "that is not the same thing!" But why isn't it?

If you are the "Christian" who happens to "identify" as "Black" and you also find yourself as a BLM activist, I want you to pause for a second to consider the very hypocrisy you have allowed yourself to manifest. I'm no saint, don't claim to be, and am not trying to be. But let's call a spade a spade here. For me, the chanting that all lives matter was the voice of reason coming to the table or the public square. They acknowledge that there may be some racial injustice or racially motivated killings towards Blacks by White cops, but to try and marginalize every other ethnic group with a singular focus of just Black people killed by cops defeats the purpose of soliciting unification and perhaps help from others to actuate change. When I hear all lives matter, I hear the hypocrisy being subtly called out towards the chanters of BLM groups. When I hear "All lives matter," I actually laugh to myself—sometimes out loud. Do they? Really?

NO LIVES MATTER

This may be said in jest or out of sarcasm but there is actual truth to the statement. Let's think about this for a second. You may not want to, but it is necessary. We are conceived, we are born, we live our life—doing whatever it is we were called to do—for however long, then we die. We are mourned briefly (*subjective*), we are moved on from, then subsequently we are forgotten about—unless we were truly extraordinary and contributed immensely to society, for which we are enshrined in history books or some random museum somewhere—if you're lucky, you get a street named after you. *Speaking of which,* isn't it ironic how every Martin Luther King Boulevard in all the major cities that have one is run down and looks like crap? It tells you what these communities think about him.

Anyways, as I was saying: If lives of any sort mattered to anyone, we would make a conscious effort to preserve them to the best of our abilities. We would not seek the death penalty, we would not eat meat—or each other for that matter. We would die from super old age or natural causes. After all, if God thought our lives mattered, he would have made us immortal. Referencing the biblical days, lives were lived for hundreds of years—now this could be subjective and scientifically a conundrum of impossibilities, but let's entertain the validity of such stories like those of Noah, Adam, Methuselah, and Seth who lived for well over nine hundred years. Then the great flood happened and God shortened the lifespan of Man. Why? Because God was essentially sick of us. God set the barometer according to which we shall live for the rest of eternity. There was a time where you could talk to God and he spoke back—if God liked you. You could pray for something and, if you were worthy of it, you were granted such wishes. Then one day, God just shut the door and stopped talking to us folks and sent his son Jesus to deal with our shenanigans until even Jesus had enough of our crap and asked his father to bring him back home and to just leave us to our own devices.

Here we are, millennia later, and we still hang on to this thing called faith where we—some of us—believe that we can continue to pray, be as good as possible, worship God or whatever deity we choose, and that when we die, we are rewarded for being good and faithful servants. I personally believe this to be the case as well; however, I am not going to hang my hat on the possibility of great disappointment. When we die, we are placed in a coffin, box, or cremated, and our ashes sit on our loved ones' mantle like a participation trophy for life—*Thanks for playing....* We can't even return to the earth as the dust from whence we came, because we have imposed the idea of placing barriers—even in death—to keep us from returning to our alleged creation. Boy! We are some sick bastards!

Do lives really matter at this juncture? I lean toward a resounding NO. We matter at the moment. We matter in the lives of those we directly and indirectly affect. We matter where it is convenient to matter. The moment we jump onto social media, go to a party, go to work, or even pay our bills online, that is when we matter. When we reach the point of being "peopled out," we shut off communications, find a hole to crawl in, and bask in our misery for however long until we feel the need to be social again. Some people find solace in just killing themselves when they feel they have had enough of life. These are the realities we live, and we live them for a reason. We psych ourselves up with these convoluted social constructs that are laden with hypocrisies and then wonder why literally no one in other countries around the world takes us seriously when we open our mouths or type in the chat box somewhere. "These stupid Americans…."

Black lives mattering, all lives mattering, and insert WHATEVER mattering are all great for the moment, and even great if you truly aspire to trick yourself into actually believing in those things, but I would honestly challenge you to think about it when it is a matter of self-preservation and protection of loved ones or your property: Will you take them out if it was required to do so? "I would call the police!" Well, that is noble, but calling the police would mean they are likely to eliminate them from society; this does not absolve you from participating in ending one's life. How about that nice juicy steak? Did that cow's life matter? How about the grass you just cut or trampled all over? If you are non-Black or non-minority, are you going to move into that minority neighborhood and show your solidarity with that community? How about you—minority person—are you going to move into an all-white community and welcome yourself to the next community barbeque? In the words of Doc Holiday from the movie *Tombstone* (1993), "My hypocrisy knows no bounds."[57]

57 S Films, "Tombstone (1993) | I'm dying. How are you? - Doc Holliday(Val Kilmer)," YouTube, April 13, 2017, https://www.youtube.com/watch?v=BdFP0d9wKxA.

▪ CHAPTER 6 ▪

LBGTQ (LET'S BEGIN GAINING THOUGHTS AND QUESTIONS)

GENDER AND SEX

I recall a time when the terms "gender" and "sex" were used somewhat interchangeably in discussions. Gender meant you were a male or female; sex meant you were male or female—depending on the context used. *See what I did there*? But to dig a little deeper here, gender generally was associated with genitalia and commonly found on applications and forms, whereas sex referred to your biological "attributes" and sometimes was found on some applications and forms for you to check—and people would make a third option—"Yes please."

Identity within these binary positions was different back then, too. Sure, we had "cross-dressers" that identified with their femininity or felt more comfortable when dressed like a woman. Then we had the other end of the spectrum, where wearing coveralls, baseball caps, and tank-tops/"wife-beaters" was the norm for them. We called these people "tomgirls" and "tomboys."[58] [59] They were picked on and even beaten up on your local playground.

58 YourDictionary, "tomgirl," https://www.yourdictionary.com/tomgirl.

59 YourDictionary, "tomboy," https://www.yourdictionary.com/tomboy.

They, too, were also mostly accepted in society with the idea that "they were born that way." This was the 1980s and 1990s. Nothing unusual. Condemned and taboo for sure, but this lifestyle was part of everyday society and not something that was mandated to be thrust upon society as some phobia because you didn't want to deal with or be around it. Some families/cultures accepted it as a phase in the person's life and, depending on their age, they would either grow out of it or get over it. It really just boiled down to where you came from and where you were in the country/world and how these things were viewed.

Sex was largely a taboo topic as well. Depending on where you were from and how you were raised, you didn't market yourself as a sex symbol or uttered sexual innuendos or expressly discussed sexual topics freely. Once again, depending on where you were from and who you were around, this may have been the norm. When you walked down the street or sat in some public venue, you knew distinctively who was a woman and who was a man. If you engaged in discussion with them or interacted with the other person, you treated them with dignity and respect—if warranted—and based on what they were: a man or a woman. If that person felt offended because you used your manners, home training, and common sense, they would either tell you how to address them or treat them, or the interaction ended right then and there. We didn't have shouting matches or get "triggered" for "misgendering" someone. We certainly didn't get fired or canceled. We simply moved on. On the flipside, however, sexual harassment wasn't much of a thing in the 1980s and 1990s. #MeToo was more like #YouDidToo back then, as women were just as guilty of "unwanted" sexual advances or fast-talk in public spaces as men were.

Gender was loosely associated with how you carried yourself. I don't recall hearing about the spectrum of genders we have now. As I mentioned previously, you were either a man or a woman. You may have been a tomboy or tomgirl in character, you may have been gay or lesbian by sexuality, but ultimately that was it—with the rare exception of the bisexual person. Those literally were the boxes you were put in if you were to fall outside of the normal social construct of heterosexuality. This social philosophy predates modern civilization, and we tend to forget this. Having the mental awareness that you may be trapped in the wrong body, feeling uncomfortable in your skin, or having anxiety about your genitalia are all normal behaviors and thought patterns that humans have had since the BC/BCE days—or biblical days. For those who do not read the Bible and those who do, but don't know it, it was addressed back then too. So, sorry, you're not special for thinking you invented something different or new. Deuteronomy 22:5 explicitly states, "A woman shall not wear a man's garment, nor shall a man put on a woman's cloak, for whoever does these things is an abomination to the LORD YOUR GOD."[60] But people did it anyway—and still do until this very second as I am writing this and you are reading it.

There was an established social norm for men and women. We have rules, laws, ordinances, customs, traditions, and so on for a reason. Otherwise collectively known as culture. It is to keep the sanity in check. Now, we are in an age where pseudoscience has taken over—redefining and reimagining a world where you can be more than just male or female. You can be non-binary, you can be gender-fluid—whatever that means—you can identify however you please, even as a cat or dog. Normalcy be damned. There is

60 Bible Gateway, Deuteronomy 22:5 (King James Version), https://www.biblegateway.com/passage/?search=Deuteronomy%2022%3A5&version=KJV.

this argument that the left likes to use to justify these abnormalities. They say, "Well Jesus says to accept and love everyone..." First off, this gets convoluted in many ways. While the core principle of Jesus was/is to love everyone and to hate the sin but not the sinner, he did not and is not advocating for you to run up and hug your enemy while they are trying to kill you either. But, rather, in Matthew 5:44, he asks us to pray for them.[61] However, let's note that in John 14:15–31, Jesus also emphasized that if we love him, we are to "keep my Father's commandments."[62] Nor would he have said, in Matthew 7:9–29, that people can choose their own version of "good" to receive his grace—and when they are judged accordingly, they ought not to look foolish. That is why it is not our job to judge people, but to use discernment when dealing with them, based on the fruits they bear.[63] So, in other words, NO, I will not accept and love everyone. Try Jesus, not me. You all know where I am going here. I am no angel and don't claim to be a prophet; however, let's call a spade a spade.

When we decide as a society to accept or justify mental illnesses and criminal behavior as by-products of broken homes, disadvantaged communities, or even a new trend and hashtag on X (formerly known as Twitter), it leads to much larger problems. People die. Cultures devolve. People move from areas. Businesses shut down and go elsewhere—like overseas—only to exacerbate the problems at hand. Endorsing someone who pretends to be a woman or a man when they clearly are not is literally medical malpractice and contributes to a further emotional, mental,

61 Bible Gateway, Matthew 5:44 (King James Version), https://www.biblegateway.com/passage/?search=Matthew%205%3A44&version=NKJV.

62 Bible Gateway, John 14:15–31 (King James Version), https://www.biblegateway.com/passage/?search=John%2014%3A15-31&version=KJV.

63 Bible Gateway, Matthew 7: 9–29 (King James Version), https://www.biblegateway.com/passage/?search=Matthew%207&version=KJV.

and physical dysphoria that can ultimately lead to suicide, mental breakdowns, and—as we have seen of recent in 2023—homicides.[64] We ought to accept the reality that no amount of puberty blockers, hormone pills, surgeries, or dresses from Target or Ross will change the fact that you have *either* XX or XY chromosomes that determine whether you are a male or a female. Not both at the same time (*super duper rare instances*), nor is it interchangeable.

GENDER AFFIRMATION

Somewhere in the medical community, some whack job came up with the idea that providing "gender-affirming" surgeries would help the person in question affirm their identity as they seek to go through transitioning to the opposite sex. See what I did there? Once again, you cannot transition genders, nor can you magically or surgically become the opposite sex. There's this pesky thing called SCIENCE we have to contend with here! Several cases of these gender-affirming surgeries resulted in near-instant regret of going through such traumatic and extreme events. This led to irreversible medical complications, mental/psychological and physical disorders (worse than the dysphoria itself), and, in some cases, even suicide. Most of these procedures, surgeries, and medications are concentrated among our youth population between the ages of eleven and eighteen years.[65] This group barely knows anything outside of home, school, and how to communicate basic

64 Michael Ruiz, "Nashville school shooter Audrey Hale had handwritten notes on clothes, numbered anklet: autopsy," *New York Post,* July 26, 2023, https://nypost.com/2023/07/26/nashville-school-shooter-audrey-hale-had-handwritten-notes-on-clothes-numbered-anklet-autopsy/.

65 Caroline Salas-Humara et al., "Gender affirming medical care of transgender youth," National Library of Medicine, October 7, 2021, https://pmc.ncbi.nlm.nih.gov/articles/PMC8496167/.

needs—let alone if they truly want a life-changing surgery that will remove or reconstruct their genitals for the rest of their lives.

The left seems to be hung up on this notion that the idea of a "woman" is false and can't identify or define what a woman is. Case in point: Supreme Court nominee at the time, Ketanji Brown Jackson, was asked by Senator Blackburn to define what a woman is, but she could not provide a definition.[66] I understood that she was trying to sit on the political fence by not affirming womanhood, but I would have thought that as a woman—and a BLACK WOMAN—she would have proudly defined what a woman was, given her personal identity. I would have given a pass to a guy being asked that question, albeit to a very small degree. A "woman," as I would have defined it, is "A female, opposite of a male/man, who can, in normal cases, give birth to another human being, who is considered a wife to a husband (man) if married; a partner in a relationship; someone who helps where one lacks in a relationship. She is a nurturer, a provider, a fierce person who handles business when the MAN cannot or will not." That is a WOMAN in my book.

The way I see it, the idea behind the gender-affirming ideology is very simple. Beta-males and alpha-females are looking to switch their physical appearances to conform to their perceived construct of their personalities. However, once they reach the period of maturity in their lives, they come to realize that they've royally screwed up and wished they thought things through a little better or never did it all. This is why parents who are condoning these surgeries, feeding these ideas into kids' heads, and advocating for this nonsense ought to be stripped of their paren-

66 Myah Ward, "Blackburn to Jackson: Can you define 'the word woman'?" *Politico,* March 22, 2022, https://www.politico.com/news/2022/03/22/blackburn-jackson-define-the-word-woman-00019543.

tal rights. Parents who are spanking or reasonably disciplining their kids should not face any repercussions from the state or federal child protective services because it likely is very much needed. Parents know their children better than anyone else in the UNIVERSE and know when that child or children may need a boot up their rear ends. It is a FACT to me that this is where society in general went astray.

THOUGHTS AND QUESTIONING

Around 2016, the idea of adding extra letters to LBGT took flight. My youngest stepdaughter at the time came home from school and entered my home office excited to tell me that she now identifies as "questioning." I asked, "What the hell is that, and what does that mean?" She further explained that her teacher, in one of the classes, told the students that it was okay to not feel like they had to be heterosexual, and being gay or lesbian wasn't the only option. They can be "questioning," meaning that they can feel around between both ends of the spectrum to see what they like the most before committing to one sexual identity. I was immediately pissed, as you can imagine. What was the premise of this conversation? Why are freshmen being told this? I was literally confused. Luckily, I knew the principal and called him to discuss this topic. He, too, was taken aback and told me he'll investigate. The teacher was subsequently placed on a warning—given it was a DoDEA school system (Department of Defense Education Activity). This is an overseas United States military school system that, depending on location, can be—and was—severely understaffed.

"Questioning" is only one aspect of the myriads of additions made to the LBGT alphabet. Even those within the community recognize the absurdity of it and shortened it down to LBGTQ+. Even within the LBGTQ+ umbrella, the transgender community has come under fire for its aggressive agenda, making allies hesitant to stand with the group.[67] This is because there has been a growing push for drag shows, indoctrinating young children and pushing for gender-affirming surgeries among the adolescent crowd. Even the traditional gay and lesbian crowd have taken some offense at the growing number of letters, especially when some individuals advocating for pedophilia tried to immerse themselves into the group, claiming they were "just simply loving someone regardless of their age." Clever, but yeah—NO![68] [69]

LBGTQ+, in its entirety at the time of this writing, is 2SLGBT2QIAPAGqBGvP.[70] You can't make this stuff up! So in long form, you can potentially fall into one or more of these categories: two-spirit, lesbian, gay, bisexual, transgender, queer, questioning, intersex, asexual, pansexual, agender, genderqueer, bigender, gender-variant, and pangender—the last six being the "plus" communities. Now, can you understand why this WAS classified as a mental illness? It is enough to drive anyone crazy, let alone trying to keep up with it and what they mean. This also explains why there is such infighting for acceptance and inclusivity into this particular community with these various personalities. This is

67 Michael Santone, "LGBTQ community faces inner conflict," *The Advocate*, September 13, 2017, https://cccadvocate.com/7364/opinion/lgbtq-community-faces-inner-conflict/.

68 Sara Jahnke et al., "Pedophile, Child Lover, or Minor-Attracted Person? Attitudes Toward Labels Among People Who are Sexually Attracted to Children," National Library of Medicine, September 29, 2022, https://pmc.ncbi.nlm.nih.gov/articles/PMC9663395/.

69 Fox 26 Houston, "'Minor Attracted Persons' wanted acceptance from LBGTQ Community," YouTube, April 19, 2022, https://www.youtube.com/watch?v=wX-7F4NtO58.

70 CBC Kids News, "Breaking down every letter in 2SLGBTQQIPAA+ | CBC Kids News," YouTube, June 6, 2023, https://www.youtube.com/watch?v=4Fn5sKfy-vU.

perhaps why they shortened it down to help avoid the nonsense it immediately presents when one looks at it. My question becomes, do those after the + feel marginalized by their own community? Has diversity, equity, and inclusion been given to the + group of the LBGTQ+ community? Likely not.

SPORTING GENDER

The Biden administration and the Democratic Party have openly embraced the idea that biological men posing as transgender women should be able to compete in women's sports, and this, too, has caused a societal divide of epic proportions. Male athletes who performed at mediocre levels at best or barely got any coverage or publicity seemingly took to the fashionable idea of donning a bikini and changing their name to be able to "identify" as a female and enter themselves into the women's divisions of sports such as swimming, weight-lifting, and even—yes—the Ultimate Fighting Championship (UFC)![71] Shattering records and claiming championships that will virtually never be held by an actual woman again—unless women hype up on PEDs and compete to reclaim their place in their own sport against men. Or asterisks are placed next to the transgender athlete's name to denote they were a trans person and the actual woman's name is credited as the proper titleholder—I don't know; makes sense to me.

This phenomenon isn't relegated to the adult sporting world either. We are seeing growing evidence of youth sports from grade school through college pushing the agenda of allowing trans athletes to compete in opposite-sex sports. Interestingly enough, the

71 Mark Raimondi, "Transgender fighter Alana McLaughlin submits Celine Provost in MMA debut," ESPN, September 11, 2021, https://www.espn.com/mma/story/_/id/32186035/transgender-fighter-alana-mclaughlin-submits-celine-provost-mma-debut.

risks of rape, indecent exposure, or even traumatization of innocent eyes of young ladies seem to be ignored by those who push this agenda of allowing bio-men to compete with bio-women. The restrooms and showers, once a safe space, have even become breeding grounds for perverts and rapists who pose as trans women; yet, this has been brushed under the rug by media outlets.[72] Schools across America have embraced opening up women's locker rooms and restrooms to trans women as a sign of being welcoming and inclusive—at the cost of ignoring the legitimate concern for the safety and privacy of biological women. At the time of this writing, I have not come across any stories of trans men having issues with male locker rooms and restrooms. Perhaps guys welcome a physically present woman in their company as they do their thing, or perhaps trans men have enough common sense to not place themselves in such a predicament to test the waters against hormonally charged guys as they shower and dress after a sporting event. Who knows?

Why are these things a controversy in the US? Why do we not see or hear about these things in places around Europe? It goes back to the beginning of this book: We are social infants doing things and figuring things out that the rest of the world literally already solved and moved on from. Stupid Americans! These issues aren't anything new in the world. In 1966, the Olympics used to test their athletes for hormonal levels among other things to ensure that you are competing in the category based on the sex in which you are born. However, "In 2015, the IOC modified these guidelines in recognition that legal recognition of gender could be difficult in countries where gender transition is not

72 Greg Piper, "Virginia school district lets male leer in girls' locker room, use whichever he wants: complaint," MSN, September 27, 2025, https://www.msn.com/en-us/news/us/virginia-school-district-lets-male-leer-in-girls-locker-room-use-whichever-he-wants-complaint/ar-AA1NrnZp?ocid=BingNewsVerp.

legal, and that requiring surgery in otherwise healthy individuals 'may be inconsistent with developing legislation and notions of human rights.'"[73] This came as a result of a 2003 decision to allow trans athletes to compete under a stringent set of guidelines, including the following: First, athletes must have undergone sex reassignment surgery, including changes in the external genitalia and gonadectomy. Second, athletes must show legal recognition of their gender. Third, athletes must have undergone transgender hormone therapy hormone therapy for an appropriate timeframe before participation, with two years being the suggested timeframe.[74] Once again, nothing new, but also not something that was recognized or allowed prior to 2003.

PRONOUNS

Have you recently walked into a conversation that went something like this: "Hi, I'm Randy and my pronouns are he/him. What is your name and your pronouns?" Now, depending on the setting and what is going on, I may just walk away from the conversation entirely. At very best, I will give my name and nothing further. My pronouns are you're/dumb if you are asking me that—and save the whole rhetoric of you don't want to misgender, mis-pronoun, or assume what I go by. If there is nothing I am saying, wearing, or doing that is outside of the traditional generally accepted practices of gender roles, then you can rest assured that I am a man and I am a he/him.

---

73 Alexis Haigler, "Trans women vs trans men competing in Olympics," *Cry of the Hawk*, April 27, 2021, https://cryofthehawk.org/sports/2021/04/27/trans-women-vs-trans-men-competing-in-olympics/.

74 International Olympics Committee Press Release, "IOC approves consensus with regard to athletes who have changed sex," May 17, 2024, https://www.olympics.com/ioc/news/ioc-approves-consensus-with-regard-to-athletes-who-have-changed-sex-1.

You will find that a lot of people on social media are placing these pronouns next to their names, especially on LinkedIn. This typically prompts me to keep scrolling and deny connection requests. Why? Because this is the very crowd that entertains the mentally ill, cosigning that being abnormal is the new normal. For example, if you, as an employer, run across a potential hire and their pronouns were "they/them," are you seriously going to reach out to them to schedule an interview? Likely not. Why? Because you immediately see the red flag that they are mentally unstable if they are referring to themselves as they/them. This would be generally applicable to the clearly identifiable biological males and females that are using pronouns of the opposite sex. Unless you are seeking to check the diversity, inclusion, and equity box, you are very much likely to keep scrolling.

The pronoun phenomenon only came into existence to give a level of credence or comfort to those in the LBGTQ+ community—a sense of affirmation by openly and forcibly acknowledging and making others acknowledge what they colloquially identify as. Employers and managers who force their employees to adhere to using pronouns within personal naming conventions will subsequently find themselves a subject of conversation around failed leadership and enforcing toxic work environments. We need to recognize these warning signs that try to permeate into our work, school, home, and social environments and nip them in the bud before your pronouns become was/were. Just imagine that even as I am pointing out the potential factors of discrimination against those who use off-putting pronouns, those who use pronouns that conform to their biological sex become discriminated against because they are not the caliber of people some woke organization is looking to hire. After all, we are already seeing evidence of discriminatory practices taking place across the US in the name of incorporating DEI policies. Why would the use of pronouns be any different, especially when we are self-identifying ourselves for elimination from the social gene pool?

■ CHAPTER 7 ■

THE POLICE STATE

THE ALPHABET AGENCIES

It is an absolute surprise to many that the FBI (Federal Bureau of Investigation) has become so heavily involved in the lives of everyday ordinary American citizens. But why is it a surprise? Since the composition of the FBI under then-director J. Edgar Hoover, the FBI has been in people's everyday business. Remember, this goes back to the civil rights era. It became really apparent to many Americans on January 6, 2021, when the alleged "Capitol riots" or the "insurrection" took place at the behest of former President Donald J. Trump! Thus exclaimed the media. But they skimmed over or never even mentioned the presence of planted FBI agents or other levels of involvement in the orchestrated field trip to the Capitol that went awry by their own doing. The FBI testified before Congress, unwilling to confirm or deny any involvement in inciting or participating in the "insurrection," but as we would find out later, they absolutely had played a very significant role in the breach of the halls of Congress, resulting in many J6 defendants getting released from prison, while hundreds more are still incarcerated awaiting exoneration.[75]

---

75 Kerry Picket, "Wray won't say if FBI informants in Capitol riot mob: 'I really need to be careful'," *Washington Times,* July 12, 2023, https://www.washingtontimes.com/news/2023/jul/12/christopher-wray-wont-say-if-fbi-informants-capitol/.

The FBI didn't stop there. In 2021 and 2022, your local school board meetings became the target of the FBI and the DOJ at the hands and direction of the Department of Education and the NSBA, as mentioned earlier. Loudoun County, Virginia, was the first target of the DOJ.[76] Parents who were angry, violent, or otherwise voiced their concerns and opinions at school board meetings against CRT and SEL were regarded as domestic terrorists and a threat to our democracy. Of course, this was determined by a letter written by someone over at the NSBA out of concern that parents are actually standing up to them! *Clutch purses and pearls...* After national outrage from the left and the right, the DOJ rescinded this policy and issued an apology to the American public, but it largely fell on deaf ears as they continued to pursue not only private citizens exercising their First Amendment rights at school board meetings in other counties and states but also conservative-based organizations and individuals.[77]

After the leak of the draft opinion from the US Supreme Court in *Dobbs v. Jackson Women's Health Organization,* which would subsequently overturn *Roe v. Wade,* a series of pro-life centers came under attack by a group called Jane's Revenge.[78] This group firebombed, vandalized, and threatened the lives of staff members at these locations across America, while the FBI passively pursued these crimes and, in many instances, outright ignored them. However, as pro-life organizations spoke out against abor-

76 Kenneth Garger, "School board members reportedly targeting parents opposed to critical race theory," *New York Post,* March 29, 2021, https://nypost.com/2021/03/29/school-board-members-reportedly-targeting-parents-opposed-to-critical-race-theory/.

77 Josh Christenson, "House Judiciary report claims 'broken' FBI 'targeting' conservatives," *New York Post,* May 18, 2023, https://nypost.com/2023/05/18/house-judiciary-report-claims-broken-fbi-targeting-conservatives/.

78 "Jane's Revenge," Counter Extremism Project, 2023, https://www.counterextremism.com/supremacy/janes-revenge.

tion, many found themselves victims of political persecution at the hands of the FBI. The FBI conducted raids on pro-life pastors, speakers, and organizations under the guise of "other" concerns involving national security or some off-the-wall alleged crime.[79] Protestors camped out, stalked, and even threatened to assassinate members of the Supreme Court, but little to nothing was done to quell those activities. In one particular instance, however, a would-be assassin was caught near Justice Brett Kavanaugh's home.[80] There is federal law prohibiting protesting at the homes of members of the Supreme Court; this is why you see them mostly doing it on the steps of the SCOTUS in DC. But oddly, this law was ignored and not enforced. Yet Hunter Biden is still walking around free? More on that later.

SOCIAL MEDIA AND MAINSTREAM MEDIA POLICE

The 2020 election was one of the most secured elections in US election history. Absolutely no nefarious activities transpired. There was no election fraud or voter fraud to any extent. These are things that were said by intelligence officials, election officials in nearly every state, and—most importantly—by CNN and MSNBC. *Your trusted sources for news.* But, if you actually believe that, then I have iced spring water made in hell to sell you for $2.99, no tax. Anyone who challenged this narrative was ostracized and labeled as an "election denier." You were publicly denigrated by Biden supporters, and your feed was pushed to the

79 Mary Margaret Olohan, "Republicans to Hold Hearing on DOJ Targeting Pro-Lifers," House Judiciary, May 12, 2023, https://judiciary.house.gov/media/in-the-news/republicans-hold-hearing-doj-targeting-pro-lifers.

80 "Armed man accused of threatening Kavanaugh is arrested near justice's home," American Bar Association, June 29, 2022, https://www.americanbar.org/advocacy/governmental_legislative_work/publications/washingtonletter/june-22-wl/kavanaugh-0622wl/.

bottom on Facebook. And if you had a YouTube channel that remotely mentioned election fraud, your video was removed and you were given "strikes" for violation of their community standards.[81] Free speech? Not in this country. And not when it comes to the election of Joe Biden! *That would be spreading misinformation*!

Social media and mainstream legacy media suppression and oppression of the 2020 election wasn't just relegated to questioning the legitimacy of votes tallied. It extended to the cover-up operation of the scandalous bombshell of Hunter Biden and his nefarious and ILLEGAL dealings with foreign countries through shady business deals at the alleged direction and support of his father, then-Vice President Joe Biden.[82] The infamous Hunter Biden laptop story that was published by the *New York Post* was immediately censored and suppressed by Facebook and Twitter as misinformation to avoid hurting Joe Biden's presidential bid.[83] The former and current US intelligence officials took to the media to defend the suppression as "hallmarks of a Russian disinformation campaign."[84] While the FBI knew it was a real thing the entire time.[85] As more evidence and information leaked out from

81 The YouTube Team, "Supporting the 2020 U.S. Election," *YouTube Official Blog*, December 9, 2020, https://blog.youtube/news-and-events/supporting-the-2020-us-election/.

82 "The Bidens' Influence Peddling Timeline," House Oversight Committee, 2024, https://oversight.house.gov/the-bidens-influence-peddling-timeline/.

83 Laura Romero, "Former Twitter execs tell House committee that removal of Hunter Biden laptop story was a 'mistake,'" ABC News, February 8, 2023, https://abcnews.go.com/US/former-twitter-execs-house-committee-removal-hunter-biden/story?id=96979014.

84 Glenn Kessler, "The Hunter Biden laptop and claims of 'Russian disinfo,'" *The Washington Post*, February 13, 2023, https://www.washingtonpost.com/politics/2023/02/13/hunter-biden-laptop-claims-russian-disinfo/.

85 House Judiciary Committee Press Release, "Testimony Reveals FBI Employees Who Warned Social Media Companies about Hack and Leak Operation Knew Hunter Biden Laptop Wasn't Russian Disinformation," July 20, 2023, https://judiciary.house.gov/media/press-releases/testimony-reveals-fbi-employees-who-warned-social-media-companies-about-hack.

the laptop, social media users that shared, commented, and even attempted "investigative journalism" were banned, blocked, censored, and suspended from colluding platforms such as Twitter, Facebook, YouTube, and Instagram.

When then-CEO of Twitter Jack Dorsey was called before Congress for the suppression of the story, he acknowledged that it wasn't something that should have been done and shifted blame away from himself as not having any idea what was going on. *Aren't you the CEO*? His subsequent exit from Twitter as CEO brought on another CEO, Parag Agrawal, who low-key continued to work with FBI agents who were embedded at Twitter to shadow ban and suspend accounts that actively spoke out against pretty much anything concerning the Bidens and the Democratic agenda.[86] This firestorm led Tesla owner Elon Musk to put an end to the shenanigans and to buy Twitter, leading to the restoration of accounts that were suspended and enabling free speech to reign supreme. Facebook CEO Mark Zuckerberg wasn't having any of it. As he too was called before Congress about the suppression of the Biden story, he also stiff-armed any responsibility. Yet, users will still experience their pages' posts and comments being buried or suspended if they are not toeing the narrative that the tech powers-that-be want them to parrot.[87]

86 House Judiciary Committee, Letter to Parag Agrawal, March 31, 2022, https://judiciary.house.gov/sites/evo-subsites/republicans-judiciary.house.gov/files/legacy_files/wp-content/uploads/2022/03/2022-03-31-HJC-GOP-to-Twitter-re-Hunter-Biden-story.pdf.

87 TOI World Desk, "Facebook executives suppressed Hunter Biden laptop to gain favor with Biden-Harris administration: Report," *The Times of India*, October 30, 2024, https://timesofindia.indiatimes.com/world/us/facebook-executives-suppressed-hunter-biden-laptop-story-to-gain-favor-with-biden-harris-administration-report/articleshow/114784471.cms.

THE CENTER FOR DISINFORMATION CONTROL

Throughout the coronavirus pandemic, the Centers for Disease Control and Prevention (CDC) went on a misinformation and disinformation campaign to combat the truths surrounding COVID-19. The World Health Organization—funded and staffed largely by China—jumped into the fray with their protocols and guidelines for the world to follow, which were based on directives not grounded in science.[88] The National Institute of Health (NIH), spearheaded by Dr. Anthony Fauci, also issued guidelines and policies around the handling of the coronavirus, but who was at the center of blame for any and everything that went awry? President Donald J. Trump! Never in the history of pandemics, epidemics, or even a scamdemic—as COVID was—has so much blame and vitriol been aimed at one single person. The Spanish Flu of 1918 didn't get nearly as much "OMG look at what the president said…" coverage.

The guidelines that were given to the public at large were not things the president himself came up with. Let's be real and understand that he is taking advice from "experts" in these respective fields, so whatever they tell him, he's not going to question it or challenge it too much. That goes for any leader, because why? They are not the "experts"! Dr. Anthony Fauci pushed the mask mandate. Knowing full well that surgical masks, cloth masks, and even respiratory masks of the industrial kind would not stop the spread or prevent viral particles from entering the respiratory system of ANYONE, but, of course, people fell for this despite the

88 Hinnerk Feldwisch-Drentrup, "How WHO Became China's Coronavirus Accomplice," *Foreign Policy*, April 2, 2020, https://foreignpolicy.com/2020/04/02/china-coronavirus-who-health-soft-power/.

reports of Fauci's own admission in an email and interview that masks don't work.[89]

Think about it for a second. You walk into a restaurant and you're wearing a mask. You are escorted to your table or told to choose where to sit, provided "social distancing" is adhered to. You sit down and wait to order your food. When your food arrives, you remove your mask and begin eating. All the while, the virus takes notable consideration that you are trying to enjoy a meal, so it will not infect you or those who are with you at your table. This has got to be the smartest and most considerate virus in the history of the universe! What is even better is that it knows to stay a certain distance above your head so that if you happen to stand up maskless and not eating, it is fair game to infect you. And it is intelligent enough to know not to infect spaces that are accurately measured at six feet! Never mind the surfaces, never mind the likely infected person preparing your food in the back. Never mind airborne deposits on material such as clothing, tables, or anything else. Matter of fact, never mind biology 101, when you learned how viruses worked, because pseudo-science has taken over.

The CDC realized it needed to do damage control because of the myriads of conflicting guidelines they had put out to the public; so in order to circumvent what we smart people were doing, it became outlawed to speak out against established policies and guidelines from the CDC, WHO, NIH, the White House, and, of course, China.[90] You could not say that the virus origi-

89 Ryan King, "Fauci roasted as 'fraud' and 'liar' after being confronted with damning study on masks," *New York Post,* September, 3 2023, https://nypost.com/2023/09/03/dr-fauci-gets-roasted-after-being-confronted-with-damning-study-on-masks/.

90 "COVID-19 Triggers Wave of Free Speech Abuse," Human Rights Watch, February 11, 2021, https://www.hrw.org/news/2021/02/11/covid-19-triggers-wave-free-speech-abuse

nated from a lab. You could not say gain-of-function research was conducted to create the virus—although the virus has a patent number, and the smart folks in the room know that you cannot patent something naturally occurring—so there you go! You could not advocate for the use of hydroxychloroquine, ivermectin, or even natural remedies such as zinc. You had to promote taking a mRNA vaccine produced by Pfizer, Moderna, or Johnson & Johnson. More on that later. Any conflicting narrative that was set to wake Americans or even the world up was immediately shut down as disinformation or misinformation and resulted in getting banned, shadow banned, or, in some cases, pursued by authorities of some nature for "misleading" the public and being a threat to public health safety.

The Left applauded these draconian efforts by the alphabet-soup agencies. I can recall the dozens of debates and arguments I had with dozens of people about what was going on. If I didn't mention it before, I am by military trade a CBRN (Chemical, Biological, Radiological, and Nuclear) Specialist (74D) in the US Army, with over twenty years of experience, and I specialized in biological and chemical agents. My final assignment was serving as a staff assistant and advisor on CBRN affairs with NATO in Naples, Italy. I was also a CBRN instructor at the US Army Chemical School from 2005 to 2008 in Fort Leonard Wood, Missouri. So I have a very firm understanding of real science! Whether COVID was engineered, naturally evolving, or a gift from God, what we do know is that it became a very politicized and hot-button issue for over three years.

In the middle of 2022, the Biden administration, specifically the Department of Homeland Security, announced that they were creating a disinformation board designed to police the internet for what they considered disinformation and misinformation from users of social media platforms.[91] As you can imagine, *1984* didn't come to fruition as they had hoped, and they subsequently had to dissolve this idea due to the massive backlash they received from the public. George Orwell's *1984* is a classic! You must watch or read (*preferably watch*) it as it illustrates the draconian measures adopted to control the population and make the people bend to the will of an elitist authoritarian regime. Much of what we have witnessed in the last few years is reminiscent of that classic—but also a premonition of what is yet to come. The changing of language and banning the use of words—"newspeak." Monitoring of your conversation through devices that will alert authorities of anything you say against their agenda—social media and your smart phones and devices. Calls to assemble and listen to someone speak as they promote some policy or agenda—*press conferences*! Folks, wake up!!!

COVID-19 should have been an international unifier, but instead it was a divider. Wearing of facial masks, vaccines, vaccine passports, social distancing, attending church, school, or even work—all became politicized issues around the world. You were automatically labeled by political affiliation solely on the basis of the stance you took when it came to COVID-related policies. Social distancing was a joke, and anyone who did not recognize the fallacy of this should really question their intelligence level. Think about it. You are told to stand or sit three to six feet away from the next individual in line or at a place somewhere to "help stop the spread." The virus is airborne and the surfaces that were touched by the previous person weren't cleaned or changed—so what exactly are we stopping again? And, by the way, the air

91 Deborah Fisher, "Disinformation Governance Board (2023)," Free Speech Center, August 11, 2023, https://firstamendment.mtsu.edu/article/disinformation-governance-board/.

didn't change magically either. These over-the-top protocols and measures seemingly did more harm than good. It goes back to the old adage of "the treatments are worse than the disease." Hundreds of billions—if not trillions—of dollars were spent on masks, ventilators, hand sanitizers, stickers, signs about wearing masks, stupid arrows for social distancing, and much more. And, "allegedly," millions of people around the world still died. More on the alleged part next!

DEATH TO SCARE YOU

Do you recall that when you turned on CNN, they had this large box in the top right corner of the screen that showed how many people died nationally and internationally, along with the number of cases of COVID?[92] Did anyone ever notice that the numbers would "realistically" change by a few dozen every twenty to thirty minutes? Did you also notice that virtually every death—even a clear-cut gunshot wound to the head—was counted as a COVID death?[93] [94] Cancer, heart attacks, old age or natural causes, all just stopped, and COVID reigned supreme as the leading cause of death from 2019 to 2020. Even the case of the flu and common cold was then classified and treated as COVID. The term "comor-

92 Lauren Giella and Graham McNally, "Fact Check: Did CNN Remove COVID-19 Tracker After Joe Biden Took Office?" *Newsweek*, January 25, 2021, https://www.newsweek.com/fact-check-did-cnn-remove-covid-19-tracker-after-joe-biden-took-office-1564233. (This example is to illustrate the example use of the "Death Tracker" not the story itself.)

93 Sydney Shea, "New Zealand man who died of gunshot wound to be recorded as COVID-19 death: Report," *Washington Examiner*, November 11, 2021, https://www.washingtonexaminer.com/news/638142/new-zealand-man-who-died-of-gunshot-wound-to-be-recorded-as-covid-19-death-report/.

94 Maxford Nelsen, "Washington health officials: Gunshot victims counted as COVID-19 deaths," Freedom Foundation, May 21, 2020, https://www.freedomfoundation.com/washington/washington-health-officials-gunshot-victims-counted-as-covid-19-deaths/.

bidities" became the buzz word when someone who had COVID died from heart disease "The heart disease was the comorbidity, but it was COVID that actually killed them...." *Huh*?

Hospitals were financially incentivized by the government to label deaths as COVID-related.[95] But claims of this were labeled as false or simply dismissed: "No evidence of this is occurring!" In 2020, my brother Eric passed away from a brief illness that resulted in septic poisoning. Guess what the coroner tried to label it as? You guessed it, COVID! We put a stop to that nonsense real quickly. There was a story out of Florida where a person was killed in a motorcycle accident, and it was labeled as a COVID-related death.[96] You can't make this stuff up! I was living in Naples, Italy, at the time when COVID hit its all-time peak. It was difficult to move around anywhere or literally do anything. The roads were shut down. You had to have special paperwork to specify where it was that you were going, what it is that you were doing, and how long it would take, when you would return home, and so on, from your employer or some other "authority" figure. The number of deaths that were being reported there at the time seemed surreal. It seemed like it was something out of some kind of horror movie where you turn on the news and they had literally freezer trucks just full of bodies. No one could figure out what to do with them. It was tough being there during this period, especially when I was preparing for retirement and trying to get my family back to the United States. Flights were very hard to get but not impossible. We were able to finally leave Europe

95 Angelo Fichera, "Hospital Payments and the COVID-19 Death Count," FactCheck.org, April 21, 2020, https://www.factcheck.org/2020/04/hospital-payments-and-the-covid-19-death-count/.

96 Soo Kim, "Florida Man Killed in Crash Listed as COVID-19 Death, Raising Doubts Over Health Data," *Newsweek*, July 20, 2020, https://www.newsweek.com/florida-man-killed-crash-listed-covid-19-death-raising-doubts-over-health-data-1518994.

in July of 2020, despite attempted travel bans being set in place since that March.[97]

Vaccine passports became this new wave of "Gestapo" control. Reminiscent of the days of Nazi Germany, where they would force Jewish people to have papers to conduct business or to travel. You were looked at as some international terrorist if you didn't get the vaccine, let alone carry a passport to prove you had those "contaminated water shots." I didn't care, and I mandated that my family did not get the vaccines under any circumstances. The rise of fake passports and fake vaccine records hit the scene almost in the nick of time. I admit that I was tempted to partake in this scheme to avoid the detection of not having the vaccines, but I ended up not needing to because we were granted permission to fly out of the country before the rules were heavily enforced. There is no telling if I would have gotten away with it or not. I have seen fifty-fifty chances of this scheme working. Thankfully I didn't have to. And thankfully, that stupidity was rescinded before society would have reached a point of "drastic times call for drastic measures."

COVID-19's politicization devolved into two trains of thought. The first being that if you were for freedom and medical liberty—meaning no mandates and no forcing of vaccines—then you had a death wish on your hands and you essentially were a murderer because you were spreading a virus and potentially killing people. The second train of thought was to acknowledge that the virus was deadly and wear a mask or two, get all the vaccines available, and gladly adhere to social distancing and other "slow/stop the spread" criteria set forth by folks who were still traveling around giving those speeches. My thing is this: How does one spread a

97 "Coronavirus: US travel ban on 26 European countries comes into force," BBC, March 14, 2020, https://www.bbc.com/news/world-us-canada-51883728.

virus they don't have? And how does one slow and/or stop the spread of something they are not nor ever were in contact with? *What happened to the cold and flu again?* We didn't hear about slowing or stopping the spread of the flu or cold when we know when and where the flu and cold seasons struck the hardest. We never talked about masking or social distancing during those times either. The common flu proved to be deadlier than the actual COVID virus had panned out to be: When the true number of deaths from actual SARS-CoV-2 (COVID) was estimated, minus comorbidities like a gunshot wound or a heart attack, it turned out to be way more exaggerated than anything else in the modern history of outbreaks.[98] [99]

98 Nina Schwalbe, "We Could Be Vastly Overestimating the Death Rate for COVID-19 — Here's Why," Our World, April 15, 2020, https://ourworld.unu.edu/en/we-could-be-vastly-overestimating-the-death-rate-for-covid-19-heres-why.

99 World Health Organization Press Release, "14.9 million excess deaths associated with the COVID-19 pandemic in 2020 and 2021," May 5, 2022, https://www.who.int/news/item/05-05-2022-14.9-million-excess-deaths-were-associated-with-the-covid-19-pandemic-in-2020-and-2021.

▪ CHAPTER 8 ▪

I'M OFFENDED!!!

SEXUAL ASSAULT & HARASSMENT

Sexual assault and harassment do not belong to any particular part of the political spectrum. In fact, it is a misnomer to think that any social issue that has outrage associated with it belongs to a political or ideological corner. Rape or sexual assault allegations hurled at Bill Cosby, Kevin Spacey, Matt Lauer, Harvey Weinstein, and R. Kelly fueled the spread of the #MeToo movement. This movement sparked the reckoning of men being called to account for their sexual advances or attempts to court women from their past—*mostly from the distant past*! From nearly every industry, women from all walks of life—*in some cases, men too*—came forward to tell their story about "unwanted sexual" advances, harassment, or even rape that happened to them by such prominent figures DECADES ago.

The scrutiny behind these allegations was met with a simple answer: "It happened, and I was afraid to talk about it or report it." This sort of response led members of Congress to jump to the defense of women who were alleged victims of the #MeToo movement spread the phrase "Believe all women."[100] Yeah, no! This

100 Robby Soave, "Feminists Who Now Claim They Never Meant 'Believe *All* Women' Are Gaslighting Us," Reason, May 19, 2020, https://reason.com/2020/05/19/believe-all-women-me-too-feminists-biden-reade/.

dangerous mantra being pushed by media and other figureheads created a storm of people coming forward with false allegations and mischaracterized or even convoluted stories to wreak vengeance on former partners and to extort people that they felt jaded by at some point in time—DECADES ago. There was little to no legal recourse victims of the anti-men movement could take against any falsehoods told against them, aside from suing for defamation of character, libel, or slander. Most men were presumed guilty by the court of public opinion before the truth finally revealed itself—and by then, the damage to their reputation was done.

There are those who were absolutely guilty of the said accusations from women who finally came forward. R. Kelly, for example, was notorious for his inclination to lure young women around Chicago high schools in the '90s. This was pretty typical behavior by music artists of that era. They would frequent the malls, school parking lots, and even the YMCAs to pick up young groupies. Guys who were starstruck or fans may get an autographed CD/cassette or a picture/poster—this was their "hush money." Parents of these young women were equally complicit in their daughters' exploitation. Mothers would escort their daughters to these parties, concerts, events, or locations in hopes that the artists would take interest and, thus, they themselves would become victims of exploitation by the parents. It was a vicious cycle, and this extended to Hollywood and other parts of the world where quid pro quo was part of the business and an accepted practice.[101]

The fake outrage comes in when these women who—*mostly*—knowingly and willfully engaged in "whatever" with these men in exchange for contracts, career advancements, or even for self-in-

101 Jessica Hopper, "Read the "Stomach-Churning" Sexual Assault Accusations Against R. Kelly in Full," *The Village Voice*, December 16, 2013, https://www.villagevoice.com/read-the-stomach-churning-sexual-assault-accusations-against-r-kelly-in-full/.

dulgent pleasures come out and say they were either forced or didn't want to engage in such behavior decades or years after the fact, when their own livelihoods from said era have dried up and any potential witnesses or corroborators are dead and gone. *How convenient.* Had these reports been made within a more reasonable timeframe of occurrence—say, a few months, then it would be plausible and perhaps taken more seriously by fans, sympathizers, and authorities. Many of the culprits of the #MeToo movement ended up in prison, sued, or shunned from society, largely through admittance of their wrongdoings or from the insurmountable evidence against them.[102]

SUPREME COURT PICK CRUCIFIXION

In 2018, Supreme Court nominee Brett Kavanaugh faced one of the most contentious confirmation hearings in history. It wasn't because he was Brett Kavanaugh, it wasn't because he was a conservative, but largely because he was a man. The left's drummed-up imagination that *Roe v. Wade* would be overturned by him once he was seated on the bench created enough fervor in the legacy media and social media world that they had to come up with something, anything, to disqualify him from being confirmed by the US Senate. Senator Diane Feinstein came up with just what was needed at the height of the #MeToo movement: Using someone from Kavanaugh's past to accuse him of raping her while they were teenagers.[103]

---

102 Karlyn Borysenko, "The Dark Side Of #MeToo: What Happens When Men Are Falsely Accused," Forbes, February 12, 2020, https://www.forbes.com/sites/karlynborysenko/2020/02/12/the-dark-side-of-metoo-what-happens-when-men-are-falsely-accused/.

103 Jennifer Haberkorn, "The GOP wants to know why Feinstein didn't come forward sooner with Kavanaugh allegation," *Los Angeles Times,* September 19, 2018, https://www.latimes.com/politics/la-na-pol-congress-kavanaugh-feinstein-20180919-story.html.

Christine Blasey Ford was the "victim." An unsuspecting psychologist who appeared before Congress still harboring the pain and suffering, the mental anguish, the embarrassment, and all other hallmarks of a sexually assaulted victim—thirty years later. The most interesting part about Dr. Ford's testimony during the hearings was that she didn't remember the date, year, or how she was *almost* raped by Kavanaugh. But she was positive it was him, and he was at that inconspicuous party drinking beer and almost raped her in a bedroom at a friend's house. Unless you are unconscious or otherwise reasonably incapacitated during such a horrendous event, it is relatively reasonable to expect that you would remember the date—or at the very least, the year. Maybe not all the details after thirty years, but, nonetheless, the sequence of events that led to the culminating event. *The left failed to rehearse that part.*

To the astonishment of the American people, the media, and even Dr. Ford herself, she suddenly remembered a timeframe after weeks of hearings and testimonies. Her now complete recollection of events fell apart even further when Kavanaugh produced his handwritten calendar from that time period, casting doubts from the allegations made by Ford.[104] Once that hoax was dispelled, another woman came forward with a similar allegation, but Senator Lindsey Graham along with the rest of the world immediately dismissed her claims, and Brett Kavanaugh was confirmed as the next Supreme Court justice.[105] But what became of Christine Blasey Ford? Senator Diane Feinstein? Or the new

104 Joshua Barajas, "See 4 months of Brett Kavanaugh's calendar from 1982," PBS News, September 26, 2018, https://www.pbs.org/newshour/politics/see-four-months-of-brett-kavanaughs-calendar-from-1982.

105 Louie Villalobos, "Second woman accuses Brett Kavanaugh of sexual assault in New Yorker report," USA Today, September 23, 2018, https://www.usatoday.com/story/news/politics/2018/09/23/brett-kavanaugh-second-woman-accuses-him-sexual-assault-deborah-ramirez/1406607002/.

woman who came forward? All of whom fabricated and lied against someone with and through legal correspondence, and through means of seeking "justice" against their alleged attacker? Nothing. What should have happened? Kavanaugh should have sued the living hell out of all of them. That was the message the #MeToo movement needed. "Don't lie on men! Now pay me!"

BUT THAT'S NOT ALL!

Brett Kavanaugh was not the first to be subjugated to the vitriolic left's antics of lying about things and using women to advance their agenda. Justice Clarence Thomas was the victim of similar shenanigans by then Senate Judiciary Committee Chairman Joe Biden (*now president*). Clarence Thomas was set to take the place of then retiring Justice Thurgood Marshall in the Supreme Court. Squeaky-clean Thomas was revered by many in the judiciary circuit on both sides of the aisle until he was nominated to the Supreme Court by President George H. W. Bush (41).[106] Then the media circus went into a frenzy.

Any and all forms of dirt against Thomas—going back to kindergarten, seemingly—was thrown at him. He prevailed against all the silly antics and was coasting to the seat until his nomination process was jolted by a bombshell report, in which Anita Hill, a former fellow EEOC colleague, accused him of sexual harassment and inappropriate behavior years earlier. *Talk about impeccable timing, right?* She, too, came under immediate scrutiny in the court of public opinion. Labeled as a liar, among many other names, she was lambasted as one who was being used by white liberals to take down another Black man.

106 "Clarence Thomas Wins Senate Confirmation," CQ Press, 1991, https://library.cqpress.com/cqalmanac/document.php?id=cqal91-1110583.

Anita Hill did not waiver. She did not back down despite pressure from the public and despite the hours of testimony from other colleagues that countered her story. Senator Biden didn't budge either. It finally all came to a head when Clarence Thomas gave one of the best rebuttals and condemnation speeches in condemnation speech history. It was colloquially labeled "The High-Tech Lynching" speech.[107] Needless to say, Justice Clarence Thomas remains one of the most controversial figures in the Supreme Court—and often the target of the Democrats to this very second.

#BELIEVEALLWOMEN

The #MeToo movement has essentially died off after much backlash by men and women who were fervently against the idea of conjuring up the past to seek justice for decades-old transgressions. Somehow, relitigating the past actions of people according to modern-day standards became a thing. There was also much consideration of not only how ridiculous this would be but how dangerous as well. Imagine being prosecuted at the age of forty for something you did as a teenager in high school, like groping someone. The interesting reckoning from it all is the uprising of the trans women movement that has permeated all facets of society that were traditionally dominated by women. Men identifying as women have usurped the gender role and model of what a woman is and does so much so that it has effectively blurred the lines as to what a woman even means. Karma or coincidence?

The backlash of this revenge morphed into something more sinister. Some men started wearing dresses and makeup and picked

107 "Clarence Thomas Statement Before the Senate Judiciary Committee," American Rhetoric, October 11, 1991, https://www.americanrhetoric.com/speeches/clarencethomashightechlynching.htm.

up pronouns of she/her and they/them in order to strip women of their power in their unique identities as women. The idea that a man can be a woman, and men can have babies too, infiltrated into social norms to the extent that legislators are spending a majority of their day writing laws affirming and denying what should actually have been established as fundamental norms, natural laws, and scientific facts. Believing all women has become the rallying cry for trans women. They coopted the phrase from its original intent of believing a woman who has been victimized by a man to now believing a man who is a victim of not being believed to be a woman.

Now we have real women, or, as they say, cisgender women, seeking to reclaim their throne as being a woman in the same era where they once were on a united front against the patriarchy and paternalistic nature of society and its associated social norms. Feminism now consists of—in large part—returning women to womanly roles and upholding the alpha-males as their coequals.[108] Women who remained neutral through it all are wondering where their place is in this social upheaval. "Do I support trans women or do I support cisgendered women who are fighting to take back the normalcy of womanhood?" This question runs akin to "Do I commit suicide or do I fight to see another day." In all theory and reality, a woman cannot support both. At the outset, you will be seen as an ally, but eventually, you will be told to sit at the back of the bus and not speak unless spoken to, not seen unless sought to be looked at, and, most importantly, not reproduce unless that trans woman and trans man want to have a baby they can adopt or take from you. PERIOD!

---

108 Cynthia Sutanto, "Feminism is for Men, Too," Feminist Majority Foundation, December 12, 2023 "Feminism is for Men, Too," https://feminist.org/news/feminism-is-for-men-too/.

FAKE OUTRAGE

Fake outrage, like sexual harassment and sexual assault, doesn't reside on only one side of any political or ideological spectrum—or even gender, for that matter. We have seen, on social media, the hypocrisy on both sides of the aisle where they are fake-mad about issues that affected real people in real time. The Colin Kaepernick ordeal, where he took a knee during the national anthem in protest against police brutality, sparked national outrage and led to the boycott of the NFL for some period of time. In conjunction with the calls to boycott the NFL, Nike supported Kaepernick, and that led to a counterprotesting boycott of Nike.[109] Admittedly, I fell into the boycott-of-NFL phenomenon, but I did buy Nike stock, because it fell to a reasonable price before taking off again. To this day, I think I caught maybe three full NFL games since then. Perhaps interests and time are stronger factors than the protesting and political overtones.

NFL fans from all across the color spectrum pretended for a while that they were mad at the NFL and Nike. The Kaepernick–Nike endorsement prompted people to burn jerseys, shoes, memorabilia, and cancel subscriptions, but once it was viewed as a racialized issue with white supremacists at work against the NFL and Nike because of Black voices speaking out, the tone quickly changed. Hence the skyrocketing of Nike stock, season tickets being sold again, and the stadiums full. The boycotts sent a message, but the irony and hypocrisy were quite glaring. Colin's protests of the national anthem lost visibility real quick, however. For those who were against kneeling during the playing of the anthem, it was a sign of disrespect to the flag—although done silently and

---

109 Aimee Picchi, "Nike shoes burned, defaced over Colin Kaepernick's 'Just Do It' ad," CBS News, September 4, 2018, https://www.cbsnews.com/news/colin-kaepernick-nike-ad-just-do-it-shares-ad-boycott/.

without fanfare, but when Tim Tebow was accused of doing so, he and his fans saw it as praying, and that was perfectly fine and patriotic.[110] The comparison became another catalyst, prompting Caucasian fans to reconsider their stances on the boycotts and actually understand the root cause of the issues at hand.

When asked about boycotting the NFL and Nike, the biggest conundrum presented to boycotters was their willingness to boycott all the organizations and corporations that supported the NFL and Nike. The list went on from Papa John's Pizza, Walmart, Target, CVS, Pepsi, Amazon, the local stores, and so on. The answers were a resounding no. How will we live!? Where can we go to support our families and ourselves? We can't boycott everything—can we? Papa John's faced a little backlash and boycott calls for a brief moment. Then the reality struck that boycotting the NFL and Nike supporters would be futile and would only lead to a self-inflicted gunshot wound to the face.[111]

Another moment in history where fake outrage and hypocrisy ran amok on social media and the legacy media outlets was during the George Floyd riots of 2019. The left celebrated the riots and destruction of cities across America, while setting up bail funds, changing laws and ordinances to accommodate the demands of BLM activists and Antifa activists at the perils of minority communities. At first, this was welcomed with open arms as cities burned, businesses were looted, and people—particularly cops—were attacked in the streets. But something magical hap-

110 Josh Peter, "Tim Tebow not happy about 'Tebowing' being brought into national anthem protests debate," USA Today, June 8, 2018, https://www.usatoday.com/story/sports/2018/06/08/tim-tebow-kneeling-national-anthem/686533002/.

111 Andy Swan, "The Numbers Behind Papa John's Brand Devastation," Forbes, July 25, 2018, https://www.forbes.com/sites/andyswan/2018/07/25/the-numbers-behind-papa-johns-brand-devastation/.

pened. The livelihoods of those who condoned, celebrated, and encouraged the lawlessness were starting to get affected.

Protestors stormed CNN's Atlanta headquarters, smashing windows and prompting CNN anchors to make a plea for calm and civility. But days earlier, they were calling it "peaceful protests" while then CNN anchor Chris Cuomo gave a two-minute tirade on the history of protesting, justifying destruction.[112] [113] Over in Seattle, the CHOP zones (also called the CHAZ) were erected, keeping residents from entering or leaving their communities, while in Minnesota, the mayor praised rioters for destroying the city before they decided to attack city hall.[114] Others on the left saw the protesting and rioting as a form of reparation.[115] It wasn't until the aftermath, when it was time for working people to go back to work, that these communities realized that BLM and Antifa infiltrated their cities, destroyed them, and left them in a state of destitution, and that their cry for economic relief and justice for the crimes committed fell largely on deaf ears.

SJWs (social justice warriors) thought they were being appeased by the left when members of Congress began making calls for legislation and local action against police brutality and policing methods in minority communities. Anytime there was a police-related shooting toward a person of color, the justification for the

---

112 Spencer Neale, "Chris Cuomo: 'Show me where it says that protests are supposed to be polite and peaceful,'" *Washington Examiner,* June 3, 2020, https://www.washingtonexaminer.com/news/2617103/chris-cuomo-show-me-where-it-says-that-protests-are-supposed-to-be-polite-and-peaceful/.

113 Daily Wire+, "CNN's Chris Cuomo DOWNPLAYS Rioting Concerns," YouTube, June 3, 2020, https://youtu.be/oxo5DjCyKq8?si=phLOTljrb7v82kvv.

114 Lia Eustachewich, "How the Seattle CHOP zone went from socialist summer camp to deadly disaster," *New York Post,* July 1, 2020, https://nypost.com/2020/07/01/how-seattle-chop-went-from-socialist-summer-camp-to-deadly-disaster/.

115 Khaleda Rahman, "Black Lives Matter Chicago Organizer Defends Looting: 'That's Reparations,'" *Newsweek,* August 12, 2020, https://www.newsweek.com/black-lives-matter-chicago-defends-looting-reparations-1524502.

riots and threats of more riots were bellowed across the media outlets by groups like BLM and Antifa. Conservative media outlets called the bluffs of these rogue groups as they began to highlight the rampant killings of African Americans by other African Americans across the country, and the "war-torn," impoverished communities run by elected Democrats that were neither being invested in nor repaired after the riots; the silence from these groups was heard loud and clear. They didn't really care. This is not hyperbole; they literally said they did not care about those things because that was not what they were fighting for.[116] *The reference (115) validates the gaslighting that the legacy media used to only validate their own claims. Anything else was always "out of context...."*

BLM began to see a rift within its rank and file as billions of dollars poured in from around the world in support of the idea that Black lives mattered. The virtue signaling from corporate organizations, politicians, and schools began to show the world that change was coming and systemic racism was finally being exposed, and a racial reckoning was about to happen—or so everyone thought. As sub-chapters began to see the "love" coming in, they reached out to the international headquarters headed by Patrisse Cullors for money to support their communities and to help rebuild what THEY'VE DESTROYED; but those requests were ignored. BLM leaders quietly disappeared into their newly bought mansions in gated communities and on small islands while the movement went on with struggle.[117] One Minneapolis

116 Chelsey Cox, "Fact check: Quotes from Democratic leaders about riots, unrest taken out of context," USA Today, February 14, 2021, https://www.usatoday.com/story/news/factcheck/2021/01/15/fact-check-quotes-democratic-leaders-riots-out-context/6588222002/.

117 Julian Baron, "Black Lives Matter faces growing rift with local chapters over finances and transparency," Fox 5 News, December 3, 2020, https://foxbaltimore.com/news/nation-world/black-lives-matter-faces-rift-with-local-chapters-over-finances.

chapter president resigned and essentially converted to being a conservative, exposing the lies and empty promises of the higher leadership and the movement itself.[118] Let's remember that after all that went down between 2019 and 2020, literally nothing has changed as BLM, Antifa, Congress, or the general public would have envisioned it would have. We are creatures of habit, and change in the extreme is not something we are willing to take on or cope with.

TRIGGERED, OFFENDED, AND ANGUISHED

A conversation on social media between two opposing ideologies typically goes something like this:

> "What you just said offended me! Delete it now!!!" "Well, I'm offended that you're offended, and I will remove nothing!" "What you're doing is very triggering and I am getting angry." "Sounds like a personal problem. If you are triggered, angry, and offended, then keep scrolling and stop talking to me." "No, I will not! I want you to delete what you just wrote!" "I'm sorry. The last time I checked you didn't pay my bills, pay for my phone (device), nor do you take care of me in any fashion. What authority do you think you have over me?" "It doesn't matter! If I say I am offended and something you did is triggering me, then you should just stop it!" "Well, I am offended that you are offended, I am getting triggered that you are getting triggered, so who's offense and triggering is more important—yours or mine?" "Arrg! I'm reporting you and

118 Lee Brown, "BLM leader says he quit after learning 'ugly truth' about group's priorities," *New York Post,* June 1, 2021, https://nypost.com/2021/06/01/minneapolis-blm-leader-says-he-quit-after-learning-ugly-truth/.

having you canceled!" "Frankly, I don't give a damn what you do or think you can do. Have a blessed day."

If you have found yourself in a similar debate or confrontation in public—*not likely*—but on social media—*highly probable*—then welcome to the world of the offended. In this world, no matter what you say in the domain of some trending social issue, someone somewhere will take offense to what you said or will have a rebuttal to it just for the simple fact that you had a different view on the topic. Typically, this type of exchange happens over Twitter—*now X*—or maybe even on Facebook, if you're engaging in a public space or commenting in some post's comment section. The offended person typically has some indecipherable username with a profile picture of some random cartoon or their cat. When you decide to go through their profile, you find that it is riddled with retweets and reposts and shares. Rarely an original thought outside of what their pet is doing or what emotions they may be feeling on the day—*delete or block them and move on.* Don't waste your time with these people. UNLESS you are extremely bored and have a lot of time on your hands to troll such ilk—then have at it. I used to do this a lot and rather enjoyed it. Nowadays, I don't have the time or much of the energy to engage in such shenanigans. Post or comment and move on.

College campuses across the United States have gotten particularly bad about shutting down and protesting ideas and conversations they oppose. Rarely, if ever, will you find an individual willing to engage a person with an opposing view in the way that they do as a group. They will either avoid you or rant out some indecipherable series of words that will make your head hurt, then walk away. K-12 schools are having their own troubles with teachers and administrators indoctrinating kids; shutting parents out of the curriculum, especially with regard to controversial or sensitive subjects; and even grooming children to think and believe they are transgender.[119] When these school officials are confronted about these ordeals, they often deny or dismiss them as misunderstandings, and claim that parents are spreading lies and disinformation about what is really happening.

The education domain has long been dominated by those who lean left, and oftentimes, you will find that they push their ideologies in the classrooms. When they are confronted with challenging or opposing thoughts and conversation, they will play the "I'm superior to you" card by attempting to flaunt their educational credentials and claim to be a leading expert in the field. This condescending practice doesn't always work. There are parents and other teachers with equal, if not better, educational credentials, who push back against these individuals, and this is what often leads to conflict and power struggles within the education domain.

When people take offense or are triggered by the simple fact that you challenge or question the validity of what it is they are pushing, this should be the immediate signal to you that what it is they are peddling is complete and utter bullshit! They are typically minions in the swath of minions working for someone who is pushing them to push these ideas or else suffer the consequences of whatever penalties there may be. Most of the time, when you press them on these issues, they subsequently admit to not actually supporting or believing in these things themselves. A stark example would be telling a teacher with kids of their own who is pushing for universal bathrooms in schools to let

119 Brian Melley, "Mother: teachers manipulated child to change identity," Associated Press, January 21, 2022, https://apnews.com/article/business-california-gender-identity-cdb790cc3059e71e22d86b8e7b445361.

their five year old go to the bathroom with grown men inside by themselves. Or for their teenage daughter to share the high school locker room with some guys who claim to be trans women. Then their tones change real fast. Why? Because a person will push or sell anything detrimental to someone else as long as it doesn't affect them or their loved ones. *I don't think I've ever met a drug dealer who sold crack to his own mother.*

Anytime someone demonstrates that they are angry, triggered, or offended by something through social media, the challenge to that emotion can be easily achieved. The first thing to do is ask what they are exactly bothered by. Number two, ask them what the solution is. Number three, ask them what they are willing to personally invest into it. If their answers are as, or more, asinine as their response to the initial alleged offense committed against them, then you know they are not serious, and their profile and subsequent answers will validate this. Hold these folks accountable—even though they make themselves invisible to the public eye as much as possible. Trolls can be trolled. The other fun thing to do is to flag their account as spam or fake. That really gets them going. *You're welcome.* The other thing to note when debating someone or engaged in a conversation online about a topic that you know is misleading or an outright lie is this: If you offer up the truth or the actual account of the topic, and the opposing party asks you to provide sources, ask them whether they required sources when they believed the story or topic from the source they got it from. The answer will be a resounding NO!

▪ CHAPTER 9 ▪

SAFE SPACES (DANGEROUS SPACES)

PRIVACY VIOLATED

It's one thing that OUR governments around the world have covertly—*in some places overtly*—implemented systems to keep track of our every move, our conversations, what we spend our money on, and even what our interests are by what we are searching for on the internet. Most of us can't just simply wake up in the morning and decide to search up the meaning of something we may have dreamed about or were randomly thinking about without (1) Facebook showing us an ad for it moments later, (2) the FBI adding us to the no-fly list, or (3) receiving random spam calls and mailers over the course of the next few days. I am guilty of searching about things just out of curiosity or to learn about them more in detail, usually for the purpose of my talk show or just to simply be informed about them. Granted, some things should not be searched for in the public domain without a prior written statement to the local FBI headquarters giving them a heads-up that you are about to engage in questionable search activity, but hey, whatever.... The risks are yours.

Even with privacy browsers, VPNs, newer search engines like DuckDuckGo, Brave, and a few others out there, your information is still being collected and shared among companies, agencies, and governments around the world—*literally*.[120] Have you noticed that when you are on the phone talking to someone and then you get on your laptop or your web browser, and all of a sudden the very thing you talked about has customized ads for it? Better yet, how about an article that appears in your news feed related to that topic? It's not a coincidence: THEY are listening to you and targeting YOU. This is not a conspiracy theory or something designed to scare you. It's very true. Outside of using a VPN (virtual private network)—some of which collect data on you anyway—you are essentially trapped in a world where you leave digital DNA in whatever you do or say.

In the wake of the World Trade Center attacks on September 11, 2001, it seemed pretty commonplace to feel like your privacy was not invaded in the digital world. Thanks to technological advances and the Patriot Act, that has changed.[121] For the better? Subjective. For the worse? Objectively speaking—YES. While it may seem that our privacy is not invaded by the second of the day, think back to the movie or book *1984* by George Orwell and the techniques used in monitoring the population. We literally have these things in place today: cameras at intersections, drones, Alexa, your Xbox, Google, Facebook, your laptop, your cell phone, your neighbors—no matter how far they are. The list goes on and on, yet we have fallen into a state of complacency where we simply accept it and move on.

---

120 Simon Patel, "How Governments and ISPs Can Monitor Your Internet Activity?" Sidekick, https://www.meetsidekick.com/how-governments-and-isps-can-monitor-your-internet-activity/.

121 Patrick G. Eddington, "The PATRIOT Act Has Threatened Freedom for 20 Years," The CATO Institute, October 21, 2021, https://www.cato.org/commentary/patriot-act-has-threatened-freedom-20-years?gad_source=1&gad_campaignid=85808169&gbraid=0AAAAADusmudXXxKTFB2i-waj9v9clFHYI&gclid=Cj0KCQjwxo_CBhDbARIsADWpDH5YX1K2lGMexld9BG2-Vc-Y2RemTgrUSVG-YJypb2k_Al86DSnXWj4aApGGEALw_wcB.

We get excited when we are reminded of our memories from nine years ago that we totally forgot about, but Facebook didn't. Or how about that restaurant you visited last week that you forgot the directions to? Don't worry, Google Maps will remind you exactly when you last visited it and damn near what you ordered. Just when you thought you were deleting and emptying the trash on your phone of those naked pics you were sending to that secret lover of yours—nope, Microsoft OneDrive will automatically save them for you, so you will always be able to cherish those moments of indiscretion. The point here is that our privacy has been violated so much, and we have generally accepted that and continue to invest in and use the tools that keep violating our privacy. *We're so weird, aren't we?*

Someone reading this will say, "Well, I don't use the internet. I don't use social media." Well, it doesn't matter. If you are swiping that bank card, if you are walking into a store, if you are at work, you are being monitored. Your data is being tracked. Your data is being shared. Taking public transportation? So what! Driving a car? Even better! Unless you have a Flintstone car and you are using your feet to pedal everywhere, you are being tracked. Even then, it doesn't matter—thanks to facial recognition and AI software! What can you or I do about the intrusive behavior of our government and the supporting agencies and corporations? Nothing. It's too late. You don't have a safe space anymore—unless you disconnect and toss out every electronic device in a hundred-yard radius and disappear into a remote location where electricity doesn't exist. Good luck, because that pesky satellite may still find you. Oh, and check the tree branches in those lovely woods you decided to relocate to. They want to track tree growth and sapling production too...

ADVERTISING STUPIDITY

Criminals do not obey laws. This should go without saying or explanation. Anyone who has intent to commit a nefarious act, outright crime, or exact revenge for some sort of perceived injustice does not give a damn about what laws they are breaking, whose feelings they are about to hurt, or what consequences they will bear. They will simply do it and let the cards fall where they shall. This is exactly why it is utterly STUPID to say or post that a school is a "gun-free zone," "drug-free zone," and really stupid—"safe space." You are literally telling a criminal, "Hey, we can't defend ourselves, so come on in and do your bidding! We welcome it!" Posters should be posted stating that, "If you enter this property doing anything we don't approve of, you will die a horrible death!" This kind of messaging will likely get the attention of someone who has some value for their life, and they will likely think twice before entering such a facility and acting stupid. Law-abiding citizens will adhere to such warnings, rules, and laws because, well, they are law-abiding and don't want any unnecessary trouble. *Strange how that works, isn't it?*

Here in Texas, it is legal to carry a firearm without a license under a law known as constitutional carry, in most cases and places. However, establishments can post a sign restricting that right—even for the law-abiding—letting patrons know that either you can or can't by these following statutes: Texas Penal Code 30.05, which prohibits carrying a gun on the property by unlicensed individuals, Texas Penal Code 30.06, under which licensed individuals cannot carry a gun on the property, and Texas Penal Code 30.07, under which you cannot openly carry—it must be concealed.[122] Now, a law-abiding person would obey these codes

122 "Title 7: Offenses Against Property," Texas Penal Codes, https://statutes.capitol.texas.gov/docs/pe/htm/pe.30.htm.

because they do not want to lose their license or get into trouble losing their right to carry a firearm; however, someone who doesn't care about either will ignore these codes and do what they want. This is just common sense, but there are people out here who don't understand this logic for some reason.

"Well Randy, what do you do to keep places safe from guns?" NOTHING. In fact, encourage everyone to get a gun for the most part. Let the cards fall where they may. As I used to say in the military, "Let Darwinism go into full effect!" In other words, let us allow the strongest to survive. You don't hear about a person going into a police station shooting up the place do you? Why is that? You don't hear about someone going onto a military installation and attacking ARMED people? Why is that? Now, anecdotally speaking, there have been a couple of occasions where this happened. I chalk those situations up to the person who was looking to die in the process while committing as much damage as they can. Nidal Hasan, the 2009 Fort Hood shooter, was the exception to this, because he went to a soft-target location and committed his act. He knew the soldiers there would neither be armed nor would they have ready access to weapons.[123] I know this information, because I was coming back from Iraq at the time that this happened and would have been going to the same facility for our return-to-station in-processing and medical checkups.

CAMPUS CONFORMITY

Universities across this great land have implanted a false sense of security in allowing students to have "safe spaces" on college campuses. This effect has even trickled down to high schools and

123 "Tragedy At Fort Hood," CBS News, 2012, https://www.cbsnews.com/feature/tragedy-at-fort-hood/.

elementary schools. The idea that grown men and women need a personal safety net in a public setting, away from other entities, within an environment that is designed to be a conduit for the free exchange of dialogue, ideas, and conversations on a myriad of topics and subjects for the advancement of our society at large is very bewildering to me. Quite frankly, it should be illegal or very restrictive, except for students with diagnosed mental illnesses that may otherwise not be conducive to their health. These universities should set admission criteria that stipulate that the student will not organize, request, or engage in demonstrations, protests, or any other unsanctioned activity that will detract from the overall mission of the university and the educational goals of the students. Such a clause on an admission application form will almost guarantee that there will be a cohesive learning environment for all, and any desires of activism of any nature will be relegated to the dorms or other school-sanctioned facility—without encroaching on others' rights to exercise their free speech or freedom of association.

This kind of idea may sound harsh and seem to limit the students' ability to be social or push for the causes they believe in. But it does not; it actually fosters an environment for them to advance their causes and advocacy on issues in a more meaningful and accepting way. If you don't want to hear Ben Shapiro or Sunny Hostin come speak at your school, don't go. In fact, schedule a competing event that may garner the attention of like-minded people, but don't try and shut it down or demonstrate against it just because you don't like it. Safe spaces in this regard would be safe locations for one to conduct their business—whether an organized event, meeting, or even a call to action of sorts, without the undue influence, disruption, or infringement of others. That is the only safe space I would consider feasible in such environments.

There was a recent story where a student who had just graduated college came to the abrupt realization that during their time in school as an activist, they had not had the time to hone their craft for their career. When they tried to enter the workforce, they literally knew nothing about what it was they went to school for.[124] [125] Now, this isn't an anecdotal thing or some one-off situation. There are literally thousands, if not hundreds of thousands, across the globe who fit this situation. They go to these Ivy League schools, or even mediocre schools, and blink their way through, paying all that money and wasting all that time just to walk across the stage or—if in an online school—open that envelope that says they have a bachelor's or master's in SOMETHING. Yet they haven't the slightest clue as to how to get started using their degree. Better yet, they have no clue as to what to do with it. Mommy and Daddy come to the rescue once again and have them stuck into some position to hopefully give them enough to pay their debt off and enough to make it through their newfound career—whatever that may be.

This is just one type of situation college activism in overload can cause a person who is supposedly entering society to facilitate its advancement. They come into it still knowing nothing or, even worse, less than before they became indoctrinated with the "Society for Good Versus Evil"—No offense, if you actually exist out there. If the idea of safe space is supposed to foster a sense

124 Chanda Prescod-Weinstein, "Grad School Activism," Inside Higher Ed, January 17, 2019, https://www.insidehighered.com/advice/2019/01/18/grad-school-activism-while-often-necessary-isnt-substitute-technical-proficiency.

125 Tom Kuegler, "I Had Zero Skills When I Graduated College," Medium, December 17, 2016, https://medium.com/the-post-grad-survival-guide/i-had-zero-skills-when-i-graduated-college-5334ae288ae4.

of security and safety for students, then how can they engage in a civil or even a civilly disobedient society that they will be ultimately charged with going out to engage in for its advancement?

What is the purpose of the university today? Is this why more and more teens graduating high school are opting not to go to college—because of its wokism? Are these students simply avoiding a pitfall that will yield them literally nothing in return for their investment? The answer is a resounding YES. Online schools are becoming the preferred method of higher education, only because you are limited in engagement with any SJW or the MAGA crowd. Stick to the topic, do your discussion on that topic, turn in your assignments, and keep it moving. Personal engagements are invited and typically limited, unless mutually agreed upon to take it further. Clubs are online as well. So activism is really relegated to an echo chamber over Zoom or Teams. *PERFECT*!

Who exactly is behind the promotion and push for activism on college campuses? Who is behind encouraging students to have safe spaces? The answer is simple: university professors of the tenured sort and their old college buddies who are the university administrators or faculty. Think about this: If I was a college professor in my mid-fifties or early sixties, and I could potentially lose my job, my pension, and my clout—*whatever that may be*—why would I teach, coach, and mentor a new generation of people who will come along and compete to replace me? That is seemingly the mindset of these university cronies. If it wasn't, then you wouldn't have hundreds of university grads complaining that they know nothing and can't apply Universal Gender Equity and Inclusion with a minor in Cultural Appropriation Awareness in the real world, let alone make a living off it. There never was a market for it, and their parents and guidance counselors should have been honest with them and told them this up front.

My word of advice to the Left and the Right: Don't be afraid to debate, discuss, or have a simple conversation that may evolve into a complex one. Agree to disagree or agree to discuss at a later time. But for the love of God, don't shut down, shut out, or run to a safe space. This is not advancing society; this is regressing it. YOUR ancestors are literally turning their backs, rolling in their graves, and are disowning you for this behavior. This behavior will get you nowhere in life and surely will not prepare you for the real world, when you will have to deal with real people and real situations. Life is meant to be hard. Life is meant to be challenging. If it was meant to be easy, then the Bible would not have been written. There would be no gurus or life coaches, advisors, teachers, and so on, because if life were easy, anyone would be able to figure it out and get through it. Since it is not, don't try to reinvent the wheel. Just improve it.

▪ CHAPTER 10 ▪

BLOGS, ARTICLES, AND APPENDIX

YOU MADE IT!

Congratulations for making it to the last chapter. Throughout this book, you were given an opportunity to be in the mind of THIS Black conservative. We—as Black people, African Americans, Foundational Blacks, or whatever category you want to place American Descendants of Slavery, also known as ADOS, in—are not a monolith, and we all think differently. Although we may agree or even disagree on many points under the Conservative umbrella, nonetheless, we know how to agree to disagree and move on. There are many out there whom I respect, and many I don't know both personally and professionally who carry this same sentiment. We are not unicorns or unique, contrary to popular belief. We are simply just an anomaly among the sea of people who heavily lean in the opposite direction on the political spectrum based largely on geography and generationally related culture. One thing I have to tell Blacks, whites, Asians, Hispanics, and even the various Europeans that I know about Black conservatives is this: Black conservatives come from a different stripe or are cut from a different cloth. We are literally the only group in the entire world that is looked upon as "weird" because we don't walk the expected political line that has been universally accepted for Black people by the rest of the world. *Isn't there something wrong with this picture?*

Why should EVERY Black person be automatically included in one political party or one political ideology, when it is perfectly acceptable for every other group to be affiliated however they please? This is the one thing I would agree that should be considered racist. As a student of history, economics, and foreign and domestic affairs, and having served in the US Army for twenty-two years with three combat tours to Iraq under my belt, I have served in leadership roles in numerous organizations, run several companies, been politically active since high school, to which my own politically driven podcast will attest. What exactly qualifies me to be relegated to being a Democrat? Just because I'm Black? *That's racist*!

Why is it racist? Because you are telling me that I cannot think, analyze, or have a varying perspective or point of view outside of what Blacks are told to have. In other words, I am generally incapable of independence as were my once enslaved ancestors who were looked upon as inferior because they were relegated to a condition of self-inefficiency, and thus, had to rely upon others (slave owners) for benevolence. But, what about those Blacks who never experienced slavery during the slavery era in America? *Don't answer that*! If I, or other Blacks, step outside this box, then we are a bootlicker, a coon, or an Uncle Tom. But it's okay for other ethnic groups to be politically affiliated however they want? *Make it make sense*!

This is America
July 2018

Euphoric statements are oftentimes misunderstood monikers or interpreted as a hidden message to a segment of a population. Both, of course, are subjective—after all, there are 330 million people in the US. So, what is an example of a euphoric statement? Make America Great Again comes to mind. Your immediate response to that would naturally be, "When was America ever great?" Well... once again, it's subjective to the individual and that particular time period in their life that they thought it was. Whether you are five, fifteen, twenty-five, thirty-five, or even ninety-five years old, think about that time in your life where things were just going great. Your first kiss. Your first date. Your first apartment/house. Your family. Even being able to just come and go as you pleased from your own home without being concerned with a curfew.

The 1990s were a great period in my life. Ranging from the age of ten to twenty years old, I was living the dream! No bills. No kids (until nineteen). No real life-ending responsibilities. Traveled a bit and met a lot of people. America was the place to be! Once again, that is and will always be an individualistic and subjective thing—just like everything else in life. I recall in the presidential bid by Bill Clinton in 1991, when he uttered the very same words in his campaign promises—NO ONE batted an eye. But of course, that is a distant memory and was said by a president beloved by many minorities at the time—who signed the very legislation that contributes to the imbalanced and minority-targeting 1994 crime bill. In America—THIS AMERICA—we are afforded the luxury to have selective memory and ignore history because we have created for ourselves safety nets to be able to bask in our blissful ignorance.

Memories, experiences, and culture shape who we are individually and collectively. We often reflect on "that one time..." or "way back when..." and we use that to justify our rationale or our decision-making process. It goes back to choice, and the choices we make directly contribute to the type of experience we will have and how it will shape our future. No matter what you feel, think, or believe in politically, religiously, or socially—YOUR choices and the second- and third-order effects thereof will shape you into who you are and who you will eventually become. Look at yourself now. Ask yourself, "Why am I the way that I am?" It's not by coincidence or some divine intervention. You, as an individual, came into being by choices that were made. Your very existence happened by someone's choice. You are the second-order effect of that choice. THIS IS AMERICA.

Accountability has become a standard that has fallen to the wayside in the last generation. Social movements rampantly placing blame on others for their own shortfalls, bad decisions, and even their own personal actions. Antifa wants to eliminate the voice of anyone who doesn't think or feel the way they feel. #MeToo has taken shape to make men solely accountable for mutual transgressions and taboo relationships. Taking a knee has shown the world that America's police force is the only entity responsible for the outcome of a situation when they are called upon or are trying to do their job in a free society. Accountability is a social construct that can be shaped to fit the current narrative—depending on who you are, where you come from, and the culture/environment that is being cultivated. But here is the reality—at the end of the day, you will still be held responsible for YOUR actions. THIS IS AMERICA.

Growth and opportunity are the biggest and main reasons why people choose to come to the United States of America. "The land of opportunity." "The home of the free!"—along with any other cliché you want to tack on to express one's notion as to why they choose to come and settle in this country. Immigrants from all over the world have staked their claim in this melting pot, and the combination of these cultures and backgrounds is what has established the American culture. All the way back to the first settlers from Europe, through the era of slavery, and even up until the civil rights movement, Americans have sought opportunities to grow and advance in ways that were not available or even possible in their very own native lands. Sure, opportunities vary from person to person and place to place. But one thing that holds true is that millions of people took a leap of faith to pursue a chance at whatever opportunity they could find. THIS IS AMERICA.

Allegiance and assimilation are often frowned upon in American culture today. The national anthem has become the symbol of hate toward minorities—because it was written by a person who owned slaves. The Pledge of Allegiance is viewed as a creed to be loyal to a country that isn't loyal to you. We fly the flags of our homeland from the rooftops and front porches of our homes. We have given ourselves labels of distinction to showcase that we are not holistically of this country. Whether you are African American, Asian American, Latin American, Irish American, or Native American, when you cross the vast waters that enter into different continents, you are nothing more than AMERICAN. In our short 243-year history, Americans have established themselves around the world as a unique entity. Nothing could be further from the truth—we are in our infancy with our "problems" as compared to the rest of the world. Our way of life reminds the rest of the world that we are a bunch of adolescents running amok in the halls of the school on Senior Ditch Day. Nonetheless, they admire our determination, our will, our resourcefulness, and, most of all, our leadership. The liberties we take for granted and the rights we have others desire and only dream of—these things seem like natural God-given things. THIS IS AMERICA.

When you go to bed tonight or sit in your car and ponder over the oppression, the injustices, the liberties, and the rights that were/are violated, stop and look at what you are doing and about to do and be grateful that you have the ability and choice to do it. Because not all have the luxury to do so. Whether you have a conservative, progressive, independent, Republican, or Democratic mindset and belief system, just remember: not everyone does. You may hate some of the things or all of the things that constitute America—but deep down inside, ask yourself two questions: "Why haven't I left yet?" and "Why are people still coming here?" THIS IS AMERICA.

How Did We Get Here?
2021

When I retired from the United States Army in September of 2020 after twenty-two years of service, I thought I would enjoy some fishing, video games, traveling, and much-needed time with my family. When the November presidential elections happened, I went to bed in the wee hours of the night, thinking I was going to wake up with President Donald J. Trump still being president. To my utter dismay, he was not, and we were to usher in President-elect Joseph R. Biden. What in the world had happened? How did this happen? Who allowed this to happen? This series of questions ran through my head for hours on November 3. Pondering what will become of America and what this radicalized Congress would do to this nation, I began thinking hard as to how and what I could do to help stave off what appeared to be the inevitable—the downfall of the greatest nation on earth.

I knew I was going to go into politics eventually—perhaps in 2024 or 2026. This has been a long-lived dream of mine—after all, I am a political science grad student, and I have a divine love for politics. I talked it over with my wife, and she told me to do what I felt was right since what I felt was usually unwavering anyways. That was my green light! The holidays rolled around, birthdays rolled around, and running for Congress for the "Last Frontier" was still on my mind. I sat down and began researching and learning what it took to throw my name and this new hat of mine in the ring—Candidate for the United States Congress for Alaska At Large.... Mid-March was here, and I was on the Federal Elections Commission website, making it semiofficial. Here come the website-building, phone calls, emails, and text messages about running for Congress. My great friend and network founder of TECN told me, "God told you, now you must do it." I reassured him that my commitment to the station remained unchanged and that I will still be part of the team through this process.

Being a candidate is like being on a deployment. You are often in strange environments, you can be among friendlies or enemies, but either way, you have a mission to do, and you must do it well with what you have at your disposal. How hard can it be for a senior noncommissioned officer with three combat tours, six children, and ten younger siblings, who interacts round the clock with people with ulterior motives? It sort of reminds me of my days working at Joint Force Command Naples—one of NATO's headquarters—during my last three years in the army. Fun, yet irritating at times. As I have trekked this course of vying for a position to represent a population of over 736 thousand citizens, I am often reminded of my time as the district and post commander of the Veterans of Foreign Wars, Department of Europe, because I am listening, learning, and leading people who are depending on me to do the right thing and make the right

America's Complacency 2023

The United States is currently in an era that most of the world thought was impossible: complacency. Our freedoms and liberties have allowed us to settle into a mindset that we have become invincible on the world stage and that the internal issues we have will fix themselves. Now, the US has become the laughingstock of the world for truly one simple reason. We've gotten complacent. The US interdiction in the Middle East for the last thirty years; our soft-power stances with China and Russia—allowing them to flex their power on unsuspecting continents and countries like Africa and Ukraine; the minority voices in social justice movements dominating our legislatures, education systems, and our nuclear family structures—all in the name of "systemic racism." The multitude of complex issues facing the United States has been undergirded, and often ignored, for so long that we have simply lost the willpower and the knowledge to effectively respond to these crises as they arise. The easiest solution has been to "let it be" or "let's see what happens." Now that we have allowed these things to come to fruition without course-correcting mechanisms in place, we have subjugated ourselves to a free-falling country—one that is becoming enshrined in Marxist-Socialist policies and agendas. After all, we have been told that we have no business being involved in our children's education, and any attempts to do so should be classified as domestic terrorism. So...because I don't want my children to be told they are inferior because of their skin color, and that all white people are racist, should I be likened to Bashar al-Assad or the Taliban? Noted.

I remember a time when a wise man told me, "Freedom is never more than one generation away from extinction. We didn't pass it to our children in the bloodstream. It must be fought for, protected, and handed on for them to do the same, or one day we will spend our sunset years telling our children and our children's children what it was once like in the United States where men were free." Ronald Reagan was ahead of his time, surely, or he was related to Nostradamus because we are in a time where this generation has allowed our freedoms to be stripped away from us in the name of, and due to, a "pandemic" and "mandates" with notable exceptions of enforcements—what I would call "Articles of Rules for Thee and Not Me." Our complacency has allowed for these things to transpire; however, we are not really pushing back against them. We're merely whispering opinions that put us in Facebook jail for a few days. Maybe Americans are tired of being free? Perhaps we are facing a reckoning for our past sins? In either case, in the matters at hand, we are complacent in far too great a number to correct the course.

During my short stint in Italy, I would frequent various historical sites and locations that were off the beaten path to explore cultures and lifestyles of the days of old—locations such as Pompeii or the enclaves of the Jewish people during and prior to World War II in Venice. Times were so much simpler back then. No instant messenger, no social media to bog your day down with entertaining yet noneducational materials; you actually had to physically interact with and communicate with one another to get anything of substance done. Now, we have DoorDash: "Leave it at my door." And Amazon next-day delivery: "Here's the code to my house; set the bags in the hall." Ask your kid what is eight times eight and to show their work. Good luck deciphering the enigmatic construction project for the answer disguised as critical thinking. This is perhaps why Oregon is waiving math and reading requirements for high school graduation, and why, among today's "leading scholars," math is deemed racist. They screwed up the basic principles so badly with Common Core that they had to subsequently abandon them altogether. An old friend told me, and he was right, "War is peace, freedom is slavery, ignorance is strength." Damn you, George Orwell. Damn it, you were right!

There's Always Room for One More Cheechako in Alaska! 2021

Our multicultural state has, and has had, some of the most influential citizens come to live here! From Bob Ross teaching the world how to paint "happy little (Alaskan) trees" to four-time Iditarod champion Martin Buser, the first musher from Switzerland to win our most beloved sporting event! Cheechako is a name given to newcomers to Alaska. Alaskans claim ownership of the word, but its origins can actually be traced to the Native Americans down around the Columbia River in Oregon. So, funnily enough, the word itself is a "newcomer" to Alaska! Nonetheless, anyone who comes from "out of state" is considered a cheechako, and I see nothing wrong with that! Alaska gets roughly thirty to forty THOUSAND cheechakos per YEAR!

To all my fellow cheechakoes, I'm right there with you. I, too, am a newcomer to Alaska. Like so many newcomers to the forty-ninth state, I, too, fell in love with it! Some of my favorite "first times" have been in Alaska. My first breath of fresh crisp Alaskan air, first glimpse of its majestic natural beauty, first time slamming on the brakes to avoid hitting a moose—wife didn't like that too much—first time voting in an Alaskan local election (conservative Republican here), first time watching my children play in the snow and learning to snowboard in Alyeska Resort, first time catching a salmon, and so many more! First time is all it took for me to become an Alaskan! Now, another AK first for me is that I am running for the US House of Representatives for ALASKA! I, like so many others in the 907 area, want Alaska to be put first! I will go to DC and put Alaska first! Alaskans, cheechakos, sourdoughs, Alaskan natives, and Native Alaskans—united we stand! As your state representative, this Alaskan cheechako WILL be asking and getting the answer to "WHAT'S IN IT FOR ALASKA!?!"

Why MEANINGFUL Infrastructure Won't Come to Alaska. 2021

Good morning,

Last week on Wednesday, I had the pleasure of being on *The Exceptional Conservative Show.*[126] We had great discussions, and it's always fun to be on this show.

On to impeding matters. Since the start of my campaign, I have spoken about the economic hindrances hurting Alaska. One of those things is the ANILCA (Alaska National Interest Lands Conservation Act). This piece of legislation blocks off nearly 90 percent of Alaska's land from ever being developed. All in the name of preservation and beauty. Alaskans have grown to accept that roads, bridges, and highways—REAL infrastructure—are next

126 TECNTV.com, "Is the Salvation Army WOKE Enough This Christmas?" Rumble, December 1, 2021, https://rumble.com/vq3kwr-tecntv.com-is-the-salvation-army-woke-enough-this-christmas.html.

to impossible to come to Alaska and bring the Last Frontier into the twenty-first century of travel, import, and export. Here is a brief excerpt from the Magnuson–Stevens Act so that you have an idea of what I will be fighting to change:

> "Gates of the Arctic National Park, containing approximately seven million fifty-two thousand acres of public lands, Gates of the Arctic National Preserve, containing approximately nine hundred thousand acres of Federal lands, as generally depicted on map numbered GAAR-90,011, and dated July 1980. The park and preserve shall be managed for the following purposes, among others: To maintain the wild and undeveloped character of the area, including opportunities for visitors to experience solitude, and scenic beauty of the mountains, forelands, rivers, lakes, and other natural features; to provide continued opportunities, including reasonable access, for mountain climbing, mountaineering, and other wilderness recreational activities; and to protect habitat for and the populations of, fish and wildlife, including, but not limited to, caribou, grizzly bears, Dall sheep, moose, wolves, and raptorial birds. Subsistence uses by local residents shall be permitted in the park, where such uses are traditional, in accordance with the provisions of title VIII."

You read that correctly—7,000,052,000 acres of public land! Insane! That is literally just a portion of the act. But wait, there's more! The Jones Act, also known as the Merchant Marine Act, written in 1920, before Alaska became a state, puts a stranglehold on shipping into and out of Alaska. Within this piece of legislation, there is a requirement that "ships eligible to transport goods from one US port to another must be US flagged, US built,

US owned, and crewed by US citizens." Today, those provisions require that such ships be at least 75 percent US owned, 75 percent US crewed, and assembled entirely in the United States with all major components of the hull and superstructure fabricated domestically.

Well gee, that is next to impossible—here's who makes the boats—not the US but.... You guessed it![127] That is just a small part of it all, but one of the biggest impacts. This past week, Democrats out in Hawaii reintroduced the Magnuson–Stevens Act for reauthorization.[128] This is another marquee antiquated law that needs serious revamping. I have also harped on the dangers inherent in this bill and its lack of accountability in bycatch trawling. For decades now, Congressman Young has essentially refused to get entangled with fixing what is hurting the economic development, growth, and sustainability of Alaska. We can modernize while keeping intact the conservational principles that have endured for centuries in Alaska, making it one of the greatest places to live for its beauty, scenery, and natural resources.

When Was Jesus Born?
2022

It has been unanimously decided among the powers that be in the world that Jesus Christ was born on December 25, (6 or 4 BC). But was he? Let's think about this for a second. Matthew 2:1–23 gives the most familiar account of the birth of Jesus, but no date was mentioned anywhere in the Bible! Who exactly decided on

127 "List of the largest shipbuilding companies," Wikipedia, 2025, https://en.wikipedia.org/wiki/List_of_the_largest_shipbuilding_companies.

128 117th Congress, "To reauthorize and amend the Magnuson-Stevens Fishery Conservation and Management Act, and for other purposes," July 26, 2021, https://huffman.house.gov/imo/media/doc/Sustaining%20America%27s%20Fisheries%20for%20the%20Future%20Act_Bill%20Text_7.26.2021.pdf.

December 25, and why? These answers will likely never honestly be answered, but answers are available. *The Washington Post* has an interesting article about this ordeal as well.[129] While we may be subconsciously, or even consciously, complicit in celebrating the arbitrary date assigned to the birth of Jesus and the giving of gifts, this brings into question the dates of everything we celebrate or deal with.

Of course, providing this at this time of year when we should be reflective and celebrating the birth of Christ may seem a bit clichéd, but I promise you, it is not. In fact, I intend to shed light on the centuries-old injustice and falsehoods that have been foisted upon us. Here are some further considerations to digest this holiday season. There are a lot of countries that operate on a different calendaring system than the one we are accustomed to here in the United States. Even in the US, we have two calendar systems—the Julian calendar and the Gregorian calendar. The Julian calendar is commonly used in military communications and special operations, while the Gregorian calendar is the most widely used in the world. Yet, there are countries like Nepal, Afghanistan, Iran, Eritrea, and Ethiopia that still use their own calendar systems for special events and holidays—like the Chinese calendar.

By technical accounts—and given this revealing information, new for some and old to others—I think it is time we explore the true birthdate of Jesus Christ on the basis of the time period and calendar system of Bethlehem around 5 BC. I am willing to bet that it was not, in fact, on December 25, but more likely in November or October, especially given the environmental conditions described at the time. Introduced in 1582 by Pope

129 Joe Heim, "Why is Christmas on the 25th of December, (It wasn't always.)," *The Washington Post,* December 24, 2014, https://www.washingtonpost.com/news/answer-sheet/wp/2014/12/24/why-is-christmas-on-dec-25-it-wasnt-always/.

Gregory XIII to reform the calendaring system for all Catholic Christendom, the Gregorian calendar has replaced most other calendars used throughout the world. Perhaps the Jewish or Mayan calendars offer a more accurate depiction of where we actually are in space and time? Social constructs and social engineering can be quite interesting when we take a moment to peel the onion on it all. Merry Christmas and Happy New Year—whether you're in America, Beijing, or Canaan.

I Have a Dream
January 2019

In 1963, no one envisioned that the prophetic words from Dr. Martin Luther King Jr.'s speech, "I Have a Dream,"[130] would not only resonate but reverberate as one of the greatest speeches in HISTORY! Every year on the third Monday of January, we celebrate his life, his birth, and the blueprint of how to live together in this ever-growing diverse society. Dr. King's dream wasn't to be the be-all and end-all of discrimination, segregation, racism, classism, and hatred. Not by a long shot—however, it would mark a pinnacle in his era: Black Americans were no longer going to abide by the systems of oppression and hatred foisted upon them by their white neighbors.

The civil rights era brought about a change in political and socio-economic discourse that not only reshaped but redefined what seemingly was the American dream. Diversity and inclusion became the new hallmark incorporated into the fabric of American ideology. Those who chose to hold on to the "days of old" faded away or were forced to conform to the "changing times."

130 Neural Networks and Deep Learning, "4K DeOldify | Dr. Martin Luther King Jr. I have a Dream Speech - COLOR," YouTube, February 15, 2020, https://www.youtube.com/watch?v=o8dzxh7Ybqw.

The dream was becoming a reality—all too quickly for some, not fast enough for others. The paradigm shift of thinking and doing in society was so swift that in some areas both the oppressed and oppressor had a difficult time grappling with the newfound "freedoms" and RIGHTS that were being exercised. The 1960s went out with a bang as a decade that brought about a new type of emancipation in the South and in other parts of the country that emulated the social injustices against those of darker complexion.

The 1970s and '80s ushered in a new kind of revolution that sought for more pieces of the American pie. This came by way of creating CRT, a perverted and convoluted ideology of Marxism but only from a racial perspective. CRT isn't a new thing, as some may think. It spawned from efforts to offer civil liberties to minorities, but became a guilt-driven phenomenon that stagnated for a couple of decades, only to reemerge in 2020 as pseudo-education. The teachings and philosophy behind CRT are not only antithetical to Dr. King's teachings but also hypocritical for those who espouse and support it. In 1915, Booker T. Washington gave a speech about a certain class of people keeping the ills of racism alive for a dollar. Today, over one hundred years later, a new breed of people not only make money from the gig of racism but employ the very systems and institutions that they feel are racist to push their own agenda. In the words of Kanye West: "How sway?!" If Dr. King was alive today, I think he would have the gumption to rename his speech to "I Have Nightmares."

It's Black History Month—Nigg@!
February 2023

Catchy title, huh? Well, don't get cozy yet, there's more. February marks the time of year that we celebrate the accomplishments and achievements of Blacks throughout history. Originally celebrated as Negro History Week, Carter G. Woodson petitioned to establish this celebration, partly as a dedication to Abraham Lincoln and Frederick Douglass. The Ford administration would go on to make it an entire month in 1976: Those pesky Republicans pandering to Black folks again! Over the next two decades, Black History Month (BHM) has lost fervor in the public domain gradually—in large part because African Americans/Black people felt that their history should be celebrated every day and not relegated to one month. Morgan Freeman explains it succinctly.[131] But to appease the broader Black audience, we nonetheless have, and those who choose to celebrate by watching a litany of "Black movies"—both with or without historical context—can do so. Not sure about the watermelons and deep-fried chicken celebrations, the spades and dominoes games, or the Black-only cookouts going on. Perhaps it's too cold out, or we recognize the stereotyping that is associated with the aforementioned, so WE stay away from those things on such occasions as BHM. *WHO KNOWS*!!!?

Now that you've gotten a brief history of why and where BHM came from, let's move on to something we generally don't discuss in any circles. The emphatic use of the word "nigga." As of late—almost ironically—Joe Rogan, a UFC commentator and podcaster, came under fire for decade-old audio clips of him using the word—whether in a disparaging way or in jest—it doesn't matter. He's canceled! Well, according to the Left, who ALWAYS give a pass to their cohorts when a person of non-color uses the word. Take, for example, Hunter Biden in a tirade with his law-

131 rickey2b4, "Morgan Freeman on Black History Month," YouTube, April 29, 2009, https://www.youtube.com/watch?v=GeixtYS-P3s.

yer—who is white by the way.[132] There are countless examples of EVERY ethnic group using the word—described as a term of endearment—but no backlash against them. Why? Here's the secret! Shhhh. You see, the word nigger was used so much by racist whites toward Blacks—both enslaved and free—that Blacks decided to co-opt the word, drop the R, and replace it with an A, thereby stripping it of its denigrative use and turning it into a word of endearment, according to the Urban Dictionary anyways.[133] That is not always the case, however; nigga is also used as a noun—"That bitch-ass nigga!" is not an endearing sentiment but rather a string of adjectives to describe someone in a denigrating manner. I can only conclude that there are some conflicting and hypocritical connotations as to why the word nigga is tossed so casually into the vernacular of people from every walk of life and from every part of the world. It's just simply cool to say.

So why the outrage when whites say nigga, or even nigger? If we were to look at this from an enunciation perspective—a theory I can give some credence to—then let's look at the context of the use. Here's a theory that is most prevailing in my mind. Nigga is copyrighted by the Black community. "You must have written consent from the owners of this work, and any use of the material is strictly prohibited by law." Since nigger was taken away from whites—as if it was tangible property—and turned into a new word owned by and exclusively used for Blacks among Blacks, any use of the word outside of the domain of these parameters is simply racist. That is the penalty given for using the word if you're not Black. You're a racist! I remember in the '90s when *Chappell's*

132 Samuel Chamberlain, "Hunter Biden repeatedly called his white lawyer the N-word, texts show," *New York Post,* June 8, 2021, https://nypost.com/2021/06/08/hunter-biden-repeatedly-called-his-white-lawyer-the-n-word-texts-show/.

133 Urban Dictionary, "Nigga," https://www.urbandictionary.com/define.php?term=nigga.

Show had this hilarious skit about the word nigga/nigger.[134] Nope, no one was canceled. Not even Howard Stern when he said it—although it was in his skits in the past.[135] Those who express fake outrage when OTHERS use the word should come to the realization that their anger is built on the foundation of hypocrisy. And since the word nigga has become a staple word across the world in music, movies, streets, kitchen tables, and back-room deals, the Black community no longer has exclusive rights to the word. In fact, your copyright has long expired, and now the world is free to use the word as a term of endearment or to denigrate someone—whether it's with the A or the R at the end, under the fair-use law. Thanks for your contributions to the world, and happy Black History Month.

Why YOU Should Care About the Jones Act
February 2022

Over one hundred years ago, on the pretext that foreign vessels were taking advantage of the American trade, import, and export apparatus, Senator Wesley Jones (R-WA), then serving as the Senate Commerce Committee Chairman, introduced the Merchant Marine Act, better known as the Jones Act. In 1920, two years after the end of World War I, the act was intended to restrict the use of foreign vessels to backfill the sealift capacity of American ships that were committed to the war efforts in Europe. Having recognized this flaw in our merchant-marine transportation system, both for-

134 Comedy Central, "Chappelle's Show - The Niggar Family - Uncensored," YouTube, December 30, 2017, https://www.youtube.com/watch?v=hLOw_SzkRQ8.

135 Gabrielle Chung, "Howard Stern Addresses His Past Use of Blackface and N-Word: 'I Evolved and Changed,'" *People,* June 15, 2020, https://people.com/tv/howard-stern-addresses-past-use-of-blackface-n-word/.

eign-flagged vessels and shady lawmakers took advantage of this glaring gap in our national security at the time.

During this period, there were a lot of shipbuilding companies in the United States, so the protectionism set in place through the Jones Act made the following stipulations: "To encourage greater use of US ships: The provisions are that ships eligible to transport goods from one US port to another must be US flagged, US built, US owned, and crewed by US citizens." Today, the modification to the Merchant Marine Act now stipulates that ships be at least 75 percent US owned, 75 percent US crewed, and assembled entirely in the United States with all "major components of the hull and superstructure" fabricated domestically. I hope you, the reader, now recognize the modern-day dilemma we face.

At present, there are only roughly five companies in the US that build ships. All these companies import parts, such as the engine, hull, and other cargo-based apparatuses, from foreign countries such as China, Taiwan, South Korea, and Norway. These seaport-based countries benefit from not having to subjugate their economy to the Jones Act, nor do they have to worry so much about importing to build, as they own, manufacture, and build their vessels in their respective countries. The United States' capacity to build ships is largely defense-based. A few cruise liners were made in the US, but a very long time ago.

Alaska stands to bear the greatest economic blow from the Jones Act of 1920, because Alaska was still a developing territory at the time of its passage. Today, Alaska is a major player in the US economic trade industry with imports and exports coming into and out of its airports and seaports. Let's not even get into the strategic geography Alaska offers to the entire world, and particularly to the United States, in terms of adversarial confrontations with Russia, China, and North Korea on a continuing basis. What does all this mean for the rest of the United States, you may ask? Well, the cost of products, to start with. Products that cost literally cents to a few dollars to make cost you dollars to hundreds of dollars more to consume and enjoy. This is largely in part to the Merchant Marine Act's restrictions on the type of vessels that are allowed to transport those goods in and around the country.

States that have a relatively high cost of living now suffer the greatest due to the Jones Act. States like California, Texas, Hawaii, Florida, New York, Washington, Maryland, Massachusetts, and the Carolinas are seeing growing economic burdens—minus the inflation brought about through the Biden administration's economic policies—because of the limitations placed on the capacity of the few US ships that meet these requirements (without waivers). The economic burdens these companies endure are passed on to YOU, the consumer. How do we fix the madness? Elect and hold politicians accountable for reversing and revising the provisions in the Merchant Marine Act to meet the modern-day status quo of the US's capabilities in terms of marine-vessel-based shipping.

Reversal and revision of the Jones Act will see a significant reduction in shipping cost that is presently consumed by end users and alleviate the burden on manufacturers and handlers of seeking vessels qualified to meet the transportation requirements currently in place by federal law. Candidates running for office presently (2022) should home in on this issue, examining how it affects the districts they are seeking to represent along with their constituencies and small businesses. Sitting members of Congress may be shying away from the issue because they either benefit from the value the Jones Act provides to specific companies and countries, or because they simply don't know about it. Either way, it's time to change it and bring in fresh bodies and minds that will tackle it head on and work together to get it done.

Black America, Stop Playing Identity Politics... September 2024

American society is at a unique point in its history. The "woke movement" has been co-opted from the militant wing of Black Americans and transformed into something more—well—diverse, inclusive, and of equity. I remember a time when "being woke" was a term used to describe being awakened and seeing through the myriads of conspiracies that were in place by the "guv'ment" against Black people, and ironically, only Black people. Now, it's a term to describe anti-white sentiment and to implement policies to "correct" both racial and social injustices against anyone—I actually mean everyone—who ascribes to fitting the criteria of being socially offended by SOMETHING imposed by this alleged system of racist institutions that plagues America's systems of governance. Never mind that these very government institutions have advanced change and opportunities to immigrants, minorities, and marginalized groups since the inception of this country.

But Black America (only Black America), not any other minority group, is in a unique quandary. For the last sixty years, WE have devoted our vote, our dollars, our voice, and our blood to the allegiance of the party known as the Democrats; yet, somewhere and somehow, WE end up with the short end of the stick—actually with no stick at all. WE are content with symbolic gestures and virtue signaling of "appointments" and with being given labels, such as the "first Black or African American" for SOMETHING, and that is good enough. WE somehow dig into the basement of our soul—or the attic, if you're all high and mighty—and justify these pacifiers by saying, "Well, it's a start.... Things take time!" I couldn't agree more. Things do all have a starting point, and things do take time. But sixty years?

I'll give some examples of how WE have been placed on the backburner—colloquially, the back porch of OUR social demands. The call for reparations was replaced with supporting Ukraine to the tune of $40 billion in total logistics value and cash. Now, of course, reparations were a ridiculous idea, but that amount of money could have gone to improving schools and communities affected by all the social ills that have been alleged throughout the last one hundred years. Moving on! The open border policy is bringing in hundreds of thousands of migrants—illegal immigrants actually—who are being placed in OUR urban centers of populations (Phoenix, Los Angeles, Chicago, New York, Washington DC, Baltimore, and so on) all in the name of "We're a welcoming city; please enjoy sucking up our resources." Then, magically, during the same Biden administration, the LBGT+ community has used Blacks as the poster children of its movements, and the trans side of the house will call US transphobic if we don't immediately identify as "allies" to their cause. Ironically, the LBG side is now denouncing the T side for their activities; somehow, the Black community has embraced this under the umbrella of inclusivity.

In a recent conversation with Pastor Stephen Broden, we both identified how the Black community has been systematically used as the voice of change for the Democrats but WE got nothing to show for it. The Black churches across America have become deafeningly silent—the better word is complicit—in the wake of their congregations going woke and to the left of God's word, to which they listen attentively every Sunday morning, Tuesday evening, and Thursday evening. Funny how WE turn a blind eye to things out of allegiance. Blacks have traditionally been known as the most confused population in the US. We act/talk conservative principles and values but vote for radical Democrats and policies every single election—at a rate of 91 percent.[136] It's a conundrum I will never understand. Now, if you are reading this and you just so happen to be Black, don't be offended. Don't say "this isn't me." Don't say "he's not talking about me or my family." Don't say I am wrong. Don't say "he's a bootlicker or a coon." Just simply say "Damn! Damn, he's right. Damn, what are WE doing? Damn!" Esther Rolle—Flo from *Good Times*—there's your point of reference. Black America, stop playing identity politics; it doesn't suit us very well. Be active in your community; vote for things that make sense for yourself, your family, your community, and your country. Vote your conscience, not just your party—that you think you identify with—but take a hard look at what you are supporting and KNOW YOUR WHY.

Why Democrats Keep Saying "Our Democracy"
September 2023

When you hear Democrat-affiliated talking heads on the lamestream media outlets talking about our country in any capacity, you never hear them say "our republic" or our "constitutional federated republic" or even one that I personally dislike, "our democratic republic" (it's an oxymoron to me). I'll get into the distinctions later. I will preface this by saying, to YOU, the reader, that this is by no means an intent to insult your intelligence. However, as little as it may be about our system of government, my intention is to make you ask the question, "Why wasn't this taught in school when I was growing up?" The answer, in short,

136 Steven Shepard, "Democrats keep getting new warning signs about Black voter support", *Politico,* October 21, 2023, https://www.politico.com/news/2023/10/21/democrats-black-voters-2024-00122846

is—actually, it could be two answers—it was, and it was glossed over, and you didn't pay much attention to it. Or you went to a school that was in, or near, an urban city, and these sorts of things are generally not going to be on the subject lists of such schools. Politically driven? Perhaps. Maybe this is why so many minorities and whites who attended urban-area schools are subjected to this fallacious idea of what our government system is.

Before the era of Common Core, and before the Department of Education became woken up on steroids—which actually began in the early 2000s—fifth grade was generally the time when you began to learn about our government and how it works. Remember *Schoolhouse Rock*?[137] During this era, we said the Pledge of Allegiance, followed by listening to, or even singing, "The Star-Spangled Banner." Hint: The republic is in the pledge. Sure, by today's standards of things, you can say we were nationalists or even overtly patriotic. But in the grander sense of things, we were Americans with a sense of national pride despite our personal and societal woes. Now, we are somewhat Americans with a sense and duty to purge all things American because it is fascist, nationalistic, and reeks of something from Hitler and Nazi Germany—another talking point of the Left. But if all things American are bad, then why are so many people still aspiring to come to the United States? If things are so horrible and our institutional systems are systematically racist, then why are so many people striving to be part of these institutions and benefit from them? These questions will never be honestly answered by the purveyors of this mindset.

Back on topic! James Madison, in creating the type of government we should have, studied intensively the various governmen-

137 PlayNowPlayL8tr, "Schoolhouse Rock - I'm Just a Bill," YouTube, November 8, 2016, https://www.youtube.com/watch?v=OgVKvqTItto.

tal systems in the world at the time. While a democracy proved to be a wiser and better choice for this great American experiment, he recognized that the citizenry was relatively disengaged from the governing discourse, and that having representatives of the people who were accountable to their constituency was the more viable approach. Besides, this was also important to avoid mob rule. When asked "What they have wrought?" after the Constitutional Convention, Benjamin Franklin allegedly told a lady, "A republic, if you can keep it." In the political science world—that is my graduate study major—"democracy" is used in a dual sense: A belief in freedom and equality among people, and a system of government based on this belief, in which power is held either by elected representatives or directly by the people themselves (Cambridge University Press). A "republic" is defined as a country without a king or queen, usually governed by elected representatives of the people and a president (Cambridge University Press). Now let's contextualize the common use of democracy as stated by the left: THE POWER IS HELD DIRECTLY BY THE PEOPLE THEMSELVES. If we are going to be in the business of changing definitions and meanings, then we can be categorized as a constitutional federated republic—which is what we are as a country—with democratic principles—meaning a free and fair election system (not so much, but that's another article later). As some scholars put it: a democratic republic. "Republic" may still be the best short title, because it actually describes, full stop, what we are as a nation.

They hate to say "republic" because it acknowledges governance by elected officials. It acknowledges that the people who elect them have the power to remove them in the event of dissatisfaction with their representation or duty of office. They hate to sound like they are giving power to Republicans—believe it or not. From this moment forward, I will include RINOs and collectively refer to both sides as the uniparty. These characters don't want YOU to have a say in what is conducted in the halls of Congress or in the Oval Office. Why? Because that means that you are acknowledging the power that you have over YOUR government; in other words, it is governed by consent. Thomas Jefferson explains this in the second paragraph of the Declaration of Independence. The uniparty does not want to be overthrown and replaced by a new government. If you think J6 was actually an insurrection against the government, then I have ice water made in hell to sell to you. Although orchestrated, J6 was, at best, a visionary example of what The People can do when they are tired of THEIR GOVERNMENT. And flags won't be waved, or selfies taken. Anywho—the next time someone refers to us as a democracy and leaves it at that, you can either correct them, ask for clarification, or be complicit in their ignorance. Better yet, just conclude that they are part of the uniparty apparatus and don't want you to have a say in how YOUR government is run.

Free and Fair Elections
September 2022

In approximately thirty-five days from now, the United States will be going to the polls for the 2022 midterm elections. Sadly, I can't say American citizens or LEGAL and ELIGIBLE VOTERS. The US election system has become a free-for-all system where, if you have a pulse—or not—you can vote. I have personally grown pessimistic about the US election process and system over the years as I have lived around the country and abroad. A privilege I have acquired from my service in the military. I have seen virtually every type of process in which one should/could register to vote either in person or by mail/absentee. I blend mail and absentee because they are the same in some places and very distinctive in others.

Anywho! There are two prevailing arguments that still reign supreme in the fight for "election integrity." The first: "We have to fix 2020!" And the second: "There is no evidence of widespread—or any, in some spaces—voter fraud, so the election process is fine." Well, I have drawn some conclusions about both arguments. Fixing the 2020 window is closed in some places and, in others, it will still prove to be futile. I have asked the question: What exactly are we fixing and, most importantly, who is WE? On the flip side of the coin, if anyone is still running around TRULY believing that voter fraud did not happen, does not happen, or does not currently exist—I personally will not, and will encourage others to not, take you seriously in life. PERIOD. The Heritage Foundation[138] has a database of fraud cases. *See for yourself.* Dinesh D'Souza's *2000 Mules* paints another picture, and the book entitled *The Parallel Election: A Blueprint for Deception* by Gregory Stenstrom and Leah Hoopes should spell it out for the slow.

When you hear the term "free and fair elections," what does that actually mean to you? What does it mean to me? What does it mean, period? A person running for office must pay a fee to file to run. In some places, a person must collect signatures, and depending on what "party" you're running in, you have a different quota of signatures to acquire than others. Neither of these cases are of a free and fair nature whatsoever. Sure, we can get into nuances about administrative costs of the state or locality for the election process to take place, but I propose a dedicated budget from the state to cover that—if they want to actually live up to

138 "Election Fraud Map," Heritage Foundation, 2025, https://electionfraud.heritage.org/search.

the mantra that they proclaim to be part of our "DEMOCRACY" (see last article). Free and fair elections mean to me like what a free market does for businesses and economies. A person decides to run for office; they file, they campaign, they either win or lose. Period. Just as in business, your goods and services will make you rich or make you poor, and you close the doors and have several seats. Period. We don't need the government at any level to interfere in our business both economically and politically. But for some strange reason, we continue to allow it—in spite of who we vote for.

Back to having free and fair elections. If elections are purportedly free, then why is there so much money involved right from the candidate to the corporate back office? Everyone—literally—has a financial interest in making money, spending money, or otherwise benefiting from our election system. I personally favor the United Kingdom's election process: six months, equal airtime, and a limit on spending. Either people like you or they don't. It's really that simple. I don't sit here proclaiming I have all the solutions to our election system problems—although give me time and I could—what I am saying is that we the people have collectively identified the issues, but they are not being fixed or properly addressed. Voting should be easy, but systems are in place to make it hard—or impossible—to cheat. There are more than enough laws and regulations on the books to regulate a truly free and fair election system. We have to be accountable to ourselves and each other to want this.

The American two-party—now seemingly uniparty—system has become problematic, as forewarned by George Washington and other founders. This particular group handpicks whom they will support and who will have the opportunity to hold the coveted seats of power—once again, this is not a fair system. We the people should get to decide, not just simply participate in the formalities created to pacify us by telling us to vote for so-and-so, when—whether I do or not—it never actually mattered.

YOU, the reader, should walk away questioning our election system and the processes that surround it. On election night, the reality that every vote was properly and accurately counted to call the winner when the poll closed a few hours prior should alone raise suspicion. And it has been already revealed that certain ballots—particularly absentee and mail-in ballots—weren't even counted unless the race was close. You, as a rightful voter, should have a problem with that because people who took the time to vote are being disenfranchised from their sacred civic duty—no one should sit idly by and be okay with that. If I must pay to affix postage to my ballot, I damn sure would want it opened and counted. If not, then the state should owe me a refund if they actually believe in a FREE and FAIR ELECTION. In November and beyond, you will now be equipped with some additional motivation to be a little more involved in the election process. At least, that is my hope.

Does Free Speech Have a Price?
December 2022

This is not an endorsement of, nor support for, Kanye West's recent shenanigans toward the Jewish community or anyone else that was/were offended in recent YEARS. With that said, there is no group or individual exempt from criticism in the world. As much as we like to believe that or think these things, that is simply not the reality. Nor will it ever change. When we criticize or make "anti-whatever" comments about anything or anyone, they are purely subjective in nature. There may be some truth to it, or it could be purely fabrication. Nonetheless, stereotypes are born from observation, and they become generalizations where applicable. Take, for example, "Asians run Chinese restaurants and cleaners," "Arabs run 7-Elevens and the local convenience stores," "Black people like chicken and watermelon," "White people like NASCAR and raisins in their potato salad"; you get the point. These are all false assumptions about people of various ethnic groups, based on collective observations of what a few people outwardly express.

These are just cold harsh realities we have in society. To cry and complain about them to no avail does nothing. To invoke cancel culture on them does nothing. Tomorrow, someone else will wake up and feel or say the same thing—as will someone a thousand years from now.

Free speech and free thought aren't only embedded in our Constitution—they are embedded in the very fabric of every person's existence. The difference is whether YOU as the individual have the balls to say it publicly, privately among friends and family, or just write it down and tuck it away. Whether it's Trump, West, Jinping, Biden, Putin, Hitler, Mussolini, Stalin, Mao Zedong, Jesus, Moses, Socrates, Plato, Neanderthal man, or Cro-Magnon man—we will always have characters who will speak their mind publicly, which some other characters won't like. I believe Kanye, aka Ye's, stereotypical observation about Jewish people resonated with those of Nazi ilk, and even with other ethnic groups, like those in the Black community, because it is something that has been spoken about for literally decades. More so, for centuries. Virtually every industry in America is, in fact, run by someone Jewish or with Jewish lineage. Hitler started the Holocaust because of Jewish economic growth and prosperity. Jesus went into the temple in Jerusalem and chased out the merchants and money changers during Passover (John 2:15–16 KJV). These are just some brief examples of how speech, criticism, and even persecution isn't reserved for one ethnicity, group of people, or individual. This is also not to say that it is okay.

But at what point do we stifle speech, thought, and legitimate subjective sentiments? Does Kanye not have the right to say or feel how he does? By these standards imposed, neither did Blacks when they were enslaved and plotted against their masters. The Uyghurs in China should just deal with their persecution and hatred versus the rebels. The people protesting in Iran should just go home and put their hijabs back on. Ukraine should just let Russia take it over without a fight. All of these examples come about when people speak out for (or against) something they believe in (or oppose). Do these actions come with a price? Yes, they absolutely do. Should they? That would depend. What is the value of freedom? What is the value of YOUR belief system? Are you willing to sacrifice it all to be truly free? Perhaps Ye is willing to. Perhaps he recognizes that "to whom the Son set free is truly free indeed…" (John 8:36 KJV). *That's life...*

A Counter Argument to Brynn Tannehill November 2022

A good friend of mine sent me this article written by Brynn Tannehill denouncing Elon Musk's buying of Twitter and discussing how this particular move will help ruin America as we know it.[139] Well, after reading this article, I had no other choice but to write this response. I will address it paragraph by paragraph for easy reference.

139 Brynn Tannehill, "Why Elon Musk's Idea of 'Free Speech' Will Help Ruin America," *The New Republic,* October 26, 2022, https://newrepublic.com/article/168309/elon-musk-twitter-free-speech-ruin-america.

First, I will address the idea that restoration of free speech should not be viewed as having undesirable consequences. As someone who has sworn an oath to uphold, protect, and defend the Constitution of the United States against all enemies, both foreign and domestic, I would not expect such verbiage to be uttered. The very fabric of any democratic system is the welcoming of speech and thought with the intent of exercising civil discourse. Not the creation of echo chambers and confirmation-bias platforms designed to shutter questioning or opposing viewpoints.

I would believe countries with autocracies would serve as examples of this; however, most people who express these ideas have never been to those countries, let alone tried these mantras there. Sunlight is, in fact, a natural disinfectant. Sure, Donald Trump's words were taken out of context to fit a narrative, but nonetheless, being told to get sunlight and vitamin D seems to be a bad thing now I suppose. It is pretty evident that liberals do hate free speech, given the birth of cancel culture. Denouncing opposing views and thoughts that are incongruent to your own—these are the very foundations as to why we on the right say libs hate free speech. What is disinformation or misinformation? Comments or opinions that are opposed to what has been established by someone of higher authority? That's interesting. Because I'm sure anyone who is asked to define or even provide evidence to counter the alleged misinformation/disinformation will fail to do so. Accepting whatever is thrown at you by anyone without questioning it or challenging it should be alarming to anyone with an ounce of sense. Why do we need content moderation? If we are in a free society, we should be able to engage in speech and thought without being regulated by an unknown entity behind another screen. If the content is threatening to life or property, we should report it and move on.

Second, free speech did not cause untold deaths; actions did. I would caution against attributing someone's speech or words as the cause of death of someone or some group. This is personally abdicating responsibility for one's own actions. I would like to give credit to the human species that we are capable of making conscious decisions regardless of influential factors that may have been involved. Speaking of which, since when did Twitter—now X—and social media become the official standard for information? If I see something on social media or even in the news, depending on the source of the segment, I, as an informed citizen, will do further research before I espouse it as fact. This is something the general society has grown away from doing, and now we think social media platforms have the ordained right to tell us what information is correct and what is not. Using anecdotal examples of crimes committed by those who became radicalized on social media gives credence to why we should allow free speech, not suppress it. I would much rather see what someone is plotting and get the heads-up versus a surprise attack. Some examples: Jim Jones mass-murdering hundreds with Flavor Aid. Timothy McVeigh blowing up a federal office in Oklahoma City. Pol Pot killing millions. David Koresh and the Waco disaster. Even recently, the Uvalde school shooting. None of these instances had social media involved, and yet, these folks were radicalized to some extent.

Third, let's address the elephant in the room. Hydroxychloroquine and ivermectin were proven to work against the virus that is allegedly paid for by, and engineered by, collaborative parties from the US and China. I find it hard to believe—as does most of the world—that hundreds if not thousands of doctors would erroneously suggest a drug or two as the alternative to the alleged vaccine that is now proving to be more harmful than the virus itself, but I digress. Furthermore, why would you not question the simple fact that the ONLY cure to this virus is a vaccine, when for decades, nearly every drug on the market has served an alternative purpose outside of its intended use? Perhaps, just maybe, you are complicit with big pharma in dictating and controlling what we will take and will not take for medication? If you think a ten-year-old is capable of determining what kind of sex-change operation they should have, then I already know the answer to that. I find was the sole cause and that these people did not take the vaccine and subsequently died. No mention of possible comorbidities, no mention that many people were falsely labeled as COVID deaths for profit-gaining, no mention that some people simply could not take the jab for other medical reasons. Just that they died because they had COVID and were unvaccinated. How disingenuous! I won't even address the stats about counties that voted for Trump having higher COVID rates. What does that even mean???

Fourth, the idea that in a market of free ideas, the truth will win out is absolute. I don't even understand how this is a debatable statement. You say that "the government, media, and financial worlds in the US are controlled by a group of Satan-worshiping pedophiles who run a global child sex trafficking operation." I will take it you have completely ignored the REAL news, missed the media coverage in the last year, or simply don't want your world to cave in with the truth. Either way, I will leave that alone and say—OH, OKAY. When it comes to the 2020 elections, if you honestly believed that eighty-one million people voted for Joe Biden out of a total population of 310 million, of which many are elderly, hospitalized, incarcerated, underaged, not interested in voting, and, oh, by the way—ILLEGAL, then I have ice water made in hell to sell you. Never mind the troves of evidence and information of voter fraud that was denied being seen and heard in courts, setting up the refrain "No evidence of voter fraud." Sure, there will be no evidence when none was allowed to be presented or even heard/seen. That's an easy one. I also take it you didn't watch *2000 Mules* either. Once again, this goes back to not having your world cave in with the truth of things presented before your very eyes—so ignore it. I'm not sure how you inferred that having competing social media platforms, or even multiple platforms, will result in a monopoly of the market of ideas? If anything, having competition and multiple platforms prevents monopolies—something Facebook tried to do by buying out other platforms. Now, Meta is the umbrella parent company to the collection it has acquired. I would recommend the book *Parallel Election,* which details how nefarious activities across the country were conducted to tamper with a free and fair election. Also, there is a database by the Heritage Foundation that gives instances of voter fraud on both sides.[140] Once again, let's not be disingenuous.

Fifth, you assert that there is a monoculture being cultivated, but you are dismissive of the fact that left-stream media and nearly all the social media platforms are monocultures in terms of the bias and political targeting orchestrated by the left. You are fine with censorship of only Republicans or conservatives, yet groups like Antifa and Jane's Revenge should have free reign on social media, which these groups have used to organize and incite violence? But once again, I digress. I'm not exactly sure what you call cross-dressing MEN dancing and parading for children. I don't know what you call slogans like "love has no age" and calls for pedophilia to be an accepted category under the LBGT+ umbrella. Oh, I know—GROOMING. I will agree that no one

140 "Election Fraud Map," Heritage Foundation, 2025, https://electionfraud.heritage.org/search.

should be attacked or bullied without provocation in any space; however, no one is exempt from criticism or from being called out for nonsense that is otherwise generally socially unacceptable. When you try to normalize sexualizing children, you can expect to be a target of vitriolic attacks—and rightfully so. Most people in society take extreme positions because it doesn't directly affect them. They have no skin in the game, so they advocate for—and on behalf of—things they otherwise would not agree with if it was THEM. I'm pretty sure you're not okay with your children being subjected to exposure by grown men in underwear. I also find it interesting that you're using the umbrella of "free speech" to castigate hatred toward alleged white supremacists and nationalists—essentially giving your audience the fuel necessary to formulate anger that could be misdirected into violence. See what I did there?

Sixth, free speech laws in the US are less restrictive because it is something that is actually enshrined in our Constitution. European countries don't value actual free speech; hence, their laws repress those who criticize their governments.[141] Remember that there have been revolutions about this, and WE had a whole war about it. Google, Amazon, and Apple can have the privilege of not hosting these companies on their servers or apps, but most people who want to access these sites can do so through direct web access and bookmark it on their phones. I actually can't believe I typed that, because, living in America, why would companies censor platforms they don't like because of moderation or lack thereof? Oh, that's right: That is fascism. Never mind. You said that Twitter is robust because of the diversity of voices—

141 Eugene Volokh et al., "Free Speech in European (and Other) Democracies, with Prof. Jacob Mchangama," Hoover Institution, November 14, 2024, https://www.hoover.org/research/free-speech-european-and-other-democracies-prof-jacob-mchangama.

which is something you actually have a problem with. You don't want diversity of voices; you want voices that are gentle, nice, and conforming to your thought processes and those of the left/liberal sector. Welcoming diversity of thought actually requires hearing, receiving, and exchanging dialogue with voices you disagree with—like I am doing now with you. I quote you: "Without moderation, racism, anti-Semitism, Islamophobia, homophobia, transphobia, and the entire witch's brew of right-wing hate will quickly take over Twitter and turn it into a Superfund site just like its competitors." I find it, once again, disingenuous that you failed to mention the hatred spewed by leftists toward conservatives. You fail to mention the racist commentary made by those on the left toward Black and Hispanic conservatives. No mention of Ilhan Omar and Rashida Tlaib's anti-Semitic comments on social media. No mention of anti-Asian or anti-Black commentary from the left. I would love to see someone from the left address the discriminatory practices employed by Texas A&M against whites and Asians in the name of "diversity." I would actually applaud those in the LBGT+ community addressing how sexualizing children and pushing for trans-gendering in children is wrong, groups like Gays Against Groomers (GAG). But these things won't likely become widespread because certain individuals don't want to fall victim to cancel culture or be attacked online by trolls. So, as many do, they sacrifice their morality and values in the name of protecting feelings—and the number of followers they have.

Thank you for your service. I'm sure you had a cringing time going through the Naval Academy and having to deal with toxic masculinity and having to be a team player to have a relatively successful career. I do understand. As a Black man who served twenty-two years, I, too, had my moments of biting my lip in the circles of raging liberals that couldn't lead their way out of a paper bag with a map pointing to the way out.

Hebrews to Negroes: A Special Review November 2022

In the months of October and November of 2022 there has been this undercurrent of backlash surrounding commentary from the artist formerly known as Kanye West, now known as Ye. Just last week, the Brooklyn Nets, an NBA team, indefinitely suspended Kyrie Irving for his refusal to state whether he was anti-Semitic and to denounce anti-Semitism. Sounds eerily reminiscent of *1984*—but anyways. I was personally a bit puzzled at the controversy surrounding both situations. I did not take the media's perspective on the issues because I knew it was crap anyways. So, I discovered a video of Ye's interview further explaining his views about the Jewish community and the backlash he received for them.[142] Now, objectively speaking, I personally didn't take any issue with what he said. He expressed his wishes and desires with envy and jealousy, saying that he wanted Black people to be more like the Jewish community because of their morality and their drive for betterment. I suppose the angst comes because a Black man actually publicly said these things, or because a Black man is sending a message to Black America to be better people—generally? In either case, you, too, can say them both or either one, and you, too, will be labeled as anti-Semitic, or so I imagine.

142 @wiserebelfilms, Kanye West Interview, Instagram, October 17, 2022, https://www.instagram.com/reel/Cj1CpS3on4L/?igshid=MDJmNzVkMjY%3D&fbclid=IwAR36he25dXNyKnA8F2SFefWSy-4ysq6hlftY5UTiU2gVHGjVgNYqe63U9J8.

I will turn my attention to Kyrie Irving and his situation.[143] Mr. Irving was essentially suspended for promoting, or just posting a link to, the movie *Hebrews to Negroes: Wake Up Black America,* which is allegedly an anti-Semitic documentary that was released in 2018, following the book by the same name.[144] Now, I have two very important questions: (1) If this movie is so horrible and promotes anti-Semitism, then why isn't Amazon under fire for making it available? (2) Why have there not been any rebuttals or other works published and promoted to counter this particular documentary? If there are, I am honestly not aware of them and, since the story broke, I have not seen anything about them. This begs the ultimate question—WHERE'S THE LIE? In this documentary, which is so reviled by those in question, there seems to be a move toward protectionism from the truths revealed, rather than an acknowledgment of the "somewhat" validity of the film toward the Jewish community. I took the time and effort to devote three hours to watching the film prior to writing this article. I wanted to ensure I did my due diligence in understanding both sides of the argument. I have seen, over the years, various sprouts of the discussion surrounding "Black Israelites," "Black Hebrews," and the like. I have had conversations in the past with some who genuinely believe they are descendants of the forebears of the land, and of the biblical fathers of the world. With or without DNA, lineage, or other associated mechanisms of proof, who am I or anyone else to argue otherwise? After all, we are in the age of identifying as we choose, right?

---

143 Jack Maloney, "Kyrie Irving suspension: Jaylen Brown says NBPA has issues with requirements for Nets guard's reinstatement," CBS Sports, November 8, 2022, https://www.cbssports.com/nba/news/kyrie-irving-suspension-jaylen-brown-says-nbpa-has-issues-with-requirements-for-nets-guards-reinstatement/.

144 "Hebrews to Negroes: Wake Up Black America," Amazon, 2018, https://www.amazon.com/Hebrews-Negroes-Wake-Black-America/dp/B07P5J2RR7.

The film *Hebrews to Negroes: Wake Up Black America* makes some very compelling arguments, and I even had a difficult time disputing some of the claims made. There were some points that have been proven categorically false or incorrect, but the summation of the film was very well put together with, like I said, a very compelling argument. So I can't help but wonder at the sudden hostility toward two prominent Black figures for conveying their PERSONAL views and thoughts about (1) being like, or better than, the Jewish community and (2) acknowledging that Blacks may be true descendants of Israel. I am one who is for freedom of speech, thought, and the expression thereof, regardless of how subjective it may appear to be. This right is enshrined not only in our United States Constitution but also in our fabric as human beings. Read my previous article about that, and you'll get a greater sense of where I am coming from.

Adidas, who recently ended their business ties with Ye (Kanye West) decided to pursue their business ventures with *HIS* product line without him in the hope of profiting from it.[145] Now, call me crazy, but if you were so anti-Ye for his comments, then I would think that you would have absolutely nothing to do with his image, brands, or even ideas that you once collaborated on. But, money walks, bull$h!+ talks. Perhaps the company saw an opportunity to gain financially from Ye without paying him by pretending to care about what he actually said. Just an objective observation. I find it interesting that there is very little to no backlash about anti-Black sentiment coming out of these very same circles, though. For example, the music industry heavily promotes violence-laden rap music that normalizes the denigration of Black women and

145 Jovani Hernandez, "adidas To Sell Yeezy Footwear In 2023, Saves $302 Million Annually In Royalties Without Ye," Sneaker News, November 9, 2022, https://sneakernews.com/2022/11/09/adidas-to-sell-rebranded-yeezy-2023/?fbclid=IwAR3EDAqMcdyxnfIdydWE4zkq8hbQuRWC-b9w243wDIu4y7gW693e51noet8.

killing of Black men. That is simply categorized as "our culture." There's no canceling of celebrities—industry professionals, past and present—who made comments or even actions toward Black people that would be considered derogatory or offensive. Hell, YOU elected one as president in 2020. The American experience is one for the ages and books! We are riddled with hypocrisy. We are riddled with lies. We are riddled with the idea that some groups are better than others—when and where convenient. We are riddled with the idea that when a Black man expresses his true thoughts and doesn't toe the line of the elite, he is just crazy or seeking attention. Better yet, he needs to be put back in his place—*whatever that may be.*

Contributing Chapter for Voices Against Human Trafficking

I am Randy Purham, retired United States Army Sergeant First Class (SFC), and current candidate for the United States House of Representatives from the great state and "The Last Frontier" of Alaska. My military career spanned twenty-two years as a chemical operations specialist, and I have done three tours in Iraq. During my last three years in the military, I have had the esteemed privilege of serving at Joint Force Command Naples (JFC Naples), part of NATO, based in Naples, Italy. It was a unique assignment, and I am very honored to have gained so many friends from the international community as well as the opportunity to travel to various countries meeting and seeing so many other people and places. I am an ardent advocate for victims of human trafficking and have spent some time discussing these issues at length in political circles and while serving in the military—particularly in Fort Hood, Texas, where sex/human trafficking rings were and are quite prevalent to this very day. Human trafficking struck close to home for me a few years back when I learned that a former colleague of mine was arrested for his participation in a sex trafficking prostitution ring.[146] Fort Hood is littered with stories of human and sex trafficking; this one story only resonated with me because he (Seymore) was someone I considered a friend, and I never thought he would be involved in anything of this nature.

While I was stationed in Anchorage, Alaska, from 2012 to 2015, the "asylum" or US Refugee Admissions Program conducted by the Obama administration resulted in many Somalis being brought into the United States. Some of them were brought to Alaska and scattered throughout Anchorage's less-affluent areas. While these areas were prime locations for sex-work activity by Natives and other minority groups living in the area, it was exacerbated by the influx of Somali refugees who were seeking to make ends meet in such austere conditions that were foreign to what they were accustomed to. According to research done by the Center for Immigration Studies (CIS), between October 2000 and September 2016, "97,447 Somali refugees were admitted during that period. Most are Muslims (99.7 percent), rather young (77.44 percent are under 31 years old and 55.55 under 21 years old), with very little education (91 percent either primary or less; only 1 percent with some sort of college/university). The top five resettlement states are: Minnesota, Texas, Ohio, New York, and Arizona."[147] During the Obama administration, a total

146 Corey Dickstein, "More than a dozen Fort Hood soldiers arrested in Texas prostitution sting," Stars and Stripes, September 7, 2017, https://www.stripes.com/news/more-than-a-dozen-fort-hood-soldiers-arrested-in-texas-prostitution-sting-1.486516.

147 Nayla Rush, "Somali Refugees in the US: Terrorist Have Families Too," Center for Immigration Studies, December 12, 2016, https://cis.org/Rush/Somali-Refugees-US.

of 294 Somali refugees were resettled in Anchorage, Alaska.[148] Very rarely will you find yourself in conversation or hearing of conversations of refugee victims of trafficking, sex rings, and even coerced terrorist operations. These kinds of conversations raise too many eyebrows and tend to place the blame on government officials who participate in these resettlement programs with unintended consequences.

During this period, I was serving not only in the military but also as the junior vice commander of the Veterans of Foreign Wars (VFW) Post 10252, and as an ambassador for the Anchorage Chamber of Commerce. In conversations with community leaders, we sought solutions to curb the growth of issues that stemmed from missing/abducted children and adults, and exploitation of vulnerable individuals, such as high school students. Our efforts seemingly went unheard or were brushed off as low-priority issues due to the vast number of other issues that suffused the media during that time. It also gave the impression that any efforts to tackle these issues would result in more work than anyone was willing to deal with. Sex work was not only a taboo discussion, but in many circles, it was considered an acceptable form of work for consenting adults—at least, that is how it was regarded. What folks failed to realize was that while sex may be between mutually consenting adults in exchange for whatever or nothing, innocent children were part of this world of sex trafficking, organ harvesting, and human trafficking to other countries, such as Russia and China. Sadly, during those years, no one was equipped to handle this reality; it was just considered as "something to be looked into"—whatever that meant. Alaska has long been considered the most dangerous state for women. Sadly,

148 "Refugees from Somalia in Alaska," *Tallahassee Democrat,* 2019, https://data.tallahassee.com/refugee/alaska/somalia/all/.

this now seems to reflect the situation in nearly the entire United States, as cases of abduction, rape, and murder are on the rise in the southern border states. The policies of the Biden administration, along with gross negligence and dereliction of duty by the Department of Homeland Security Secretary Alejandro Mayorkas, have only exacerbated the problem.

While stationed in Naples, I was exposed to a stark reality that I would only have seen on television or heard about through austere foreign affairs–related conversations. That reality was of actual human trafficking conducted in broad daylight with barely anyone batting an eye to what was unfolding right in front of them. Sadly enough, it boiled down to sex trafficking of migrant women coming mainly from African countries. Prostitution is LEGAL in Italy. As well as in Germany, where you will find this activity highly regulated and contained in brothels located in cities like Frankfurt, Munich, and smaller surrounding cities close to military installations—commonly also known as "red light districts." When my family and I relocated to Naples in 2017, we arrived early summer and in time to get adjusted to the weather and the idea that air conditioning is considered a luxury that not many places off the military installation had. Opened windows and a lot of water was the key to survival in temperatures exceeding 75 degrees. We often took walks down by the Bay of Naples, an area that had a coastline stretching across the downtown area. A popular area to hop on a boat or ferry after a day of shopping and enjoy lunch on one of the neighboring islands, such as Capri or Ischia. While it is customary to do these things, it was also customary to pay—seemingly under duress—the African male attendants who sat in the parking lots of public attractions. This payment, typically around five euros, was meant to ensure the safety of your vehicle and that everything would remain intact upon your return. Otherwise, literally, even in broad daylight, your windows would be busted, tires flattened or removed, and the inside of the vehicle vandalized. And amazingly, no one would claim to see a thing!

Cheap Americans are the target of these heinous attacks. The African men who work these parking lots know the difference between touring Americans and regular local Italians. If an American is accompanied by an Italian, you have a 75/25 percent chance of being okay. It is just easier to pay the African the change—that is recommended to be kept in the center console or somewhere in the vehicle—to avoid being a victim. You may ask, why African men, and why are they doing these things? Great question. As African migrants/immigrants/trafficked persons come into the country, they are not coming with much of their own resources. In fact, many, if not all, have their resources taken upon arrival by exploiters who promise safe passage and guarantees of "freedom" from being deported or detained. Personal identification records are taken as ransom, and a fee of up to €10,000 is the debt that they incur to be freed from their exploiter's captivity. The men are then left to work on farms and in fields, in parking lots, or, for the lucky ones, in a labor industry, such as store cleaning or minor street construction. Of course, these men are paid less than standard or desirable wages, under the table to avoid payroll and taxes. Many businesses will not hire them for two main reasons: (1) They are migrants of questionable legal status and (2) they are typically undocumented. These two factors alone place business owners in a precarious position if they were to risk being associated with such Africans.

Female African arrivals have it far worse. They are mostly relegated to working the streets as prostitutes or working as maids. Living conditions for the women are typically with their exploiters or in secluded (out of sight, but easy to find if you're looking) trailer parks or makeshift shacks. Often, you will find them holding residence in abandoned buildings and warehouses—unbothered by local authorities. These women, among those of other nationalities, are transported around local towns surrounding the city of Naples to work the wooded or vegetated areas, where passersby can easily pick them up and return them to the location in a matter of minutes—all the while being under surveillance by someone on a bike or in a parked car in the event of any trouble, or if the woman was gone longer than expected. On the surface, these women seem to enjoy their line of work, as you can also find them in stores, shopping together for makeup and outfits. They do not really engage with anyone during this time as they are once again under the microscope, so any hint of trying to seek help or to get away is a futile task. Speaking with local authorities and some local friends that I made during the time, my curiosity about this covert yet overt operation was piqued. Aside from the tactics and procedures that I previously mentioned, there is the other dynamic that I did not discuss: the exploiters.

The exploiters come from various backgrounds. They are your everyday, average citizen who may work a typical 9–5 job, or someone considered a domestic engineer (house-spouse), or a stay-at-home relative. When you hear the term "mafia" or "street gang," you immediately think of elaborate networks of people with fancy cars, homes, and clothing. NO. Far from it. The mafia members that I have encountered were simple people like a bakery store worker, a custodian/janitor, a local police officer, and a schoolteacher. The prostitution "game" is only a pillar in which money is made and favors are given. Exploiting the vulnerable women is considered a win-win situation for both the exploited and the exploiter. For example, if a schoolteacher wants access to a few women, he dials the handlers to acquire them, pays a fee for the exchange, and takes the women to work for him—or someone else—and they are all paid, and the schoolteacher returns the women back to the handler after profiting from the proceeds from the women's work. Often, the amount is split according to some agreed upon ratio, like seventy to thirty. Exploiters do not stay in this business for long. Especially ones with careers or families. They will do it for a couple of years and pass on their knowledge and network to the new guy/gal who comes along. It is a vicious and never-ending cycle. "The supply will always be available, and so will the demand," said one person in a briefing to me and my fellow colleagues at work one day, in a discussion about the missing and exploited people around southern Italy.

Rescue boats and humanitarian aid vessels are among the biggest means used to bring migrants/immigrants/trafficked persons into any European coastal country. For example, in Palermo, Italy, a German aid group had a boat full of migrants, which was seized by the Italian coastguard in 2017, and the group was charged with aiding in illegal immigration.[149] While this was one of the larger operations intercepted by authorities, there are dozens more involving smaller boats and smaller groups of people, which go unreported or with barely a mention. Many of these people are subsequently let off or let into the country due to a lack of resources to facilitate a safe return to their country of origin. Although African migrants are the largest population of exploited and trafficked persons in the European sector, independent sex workers from other neighboring countries find themselves victimized in similar fashion. Women travel to "prostitution-permit-

149 Wladimiro Pantaleone, "Italy seizes NGO rescue boat for allegedly aiding illegal migration," Reuters, August 3, 2017, https://www.reuters.com/article/us-europe-migrants-italy-ngo/italy-seizes-ngo-rescue-boat-for-allegedly-aiding-illegal-migration-idUSKBN1AI21B/.

ting countries" in search of work opportunities or to get away from dire situations in their home countries. Unable to afford the relocation costs, many turn to independent sex work, where—unlike trafficked sex workers—they prostitute themselves without the "protection" of exploiters. However, when these women find themselves in trouble, either over territorial issues or with customers who may be a bit too aggressive for their liking, they turn to exploiters for help and fall into the trap of being forever indebted to their exploiter—or, as they call them, their "protector."

A lack of resources—both financial and human—are one of the biggest factors in combating human trafficking, sexual exploitation of people, and illegal immigration in countries like the United States, Mexico, Italy, France, and Germany. Foreign policy responses to these situations have also been lackluster in terms of an effective solution to curbing these activities. The prevailing arguments and reasons are that politicians and local, state, and federal authorities all benefit either financially or through other means by allowing or participating in these activities at the expense of those seeking to migrate from one place to another. It is unfortunate that this allegedly taboo discussion will not be addressed in a meaningful way—by having serious and honest dialogue about what is happening and how to fix it—because that would require someone in the room, someone sitting at the table, to take ownership of the problem and admit that their actions or inaction have exacerbated it. Often, we only hear of the perpetrators that were arrested for soliciting or trafficking, but we never ever hear of the connected network that was involved or enabled this "end product" being taken down. Why is that?

There are dozens of organizations, resources, and communities especially designed to help combat human trafficking, and there are many support groups and advocacy programs like Voices

Against Trafficking that exist to assist survivors of this egregious crime against humanity. A colleague of mine, Jon Uhler, has a website with a plethora of resources available to those who have experienced, or know someone who has experienced, traumatic events such as being trafficked, raped, or otherwise abused in any form. We, as the human community, must stand up, speak out, and apply serious pressure to our governmental leaders to do more to put an end to human trafficking and exploitation of persons. While I was serving in the military, there were two frequent sayings we would always hear when it came to accountability: "See something, say something" and "Silence is compliance." I hope that reading this book today inspires you to go forth and be a warrior for the exploited, an advocate for the voiceless, and a source of healing for the hurt. We can no longer use being naïve as an excuse for our inaction; it is time to fight. We all have three choices in life when it comes to dealing with hard issues that face us: You can give in, give up, or give it all you've got. I hope and pray you sincerely give it all you've got.

Why America Needs Donald Trump
August 2024

For over the past seven years, the world—and mainly the United States—has had to deal with a unique man, Donald John Trump. But it wasn't just the past seven years; in fact, it has been the past forty years at a minimum. DJT was, and arguably still is, the most influential person in modern history. His business prowess featured him in magazines, books, television shows, and, yes, even in rap music. Not many people know, or knew, Trump's political leanings over the years. Those who did, didn't care because, well, he's Donald Trump, the self-made billionaire who was philanthropic with his money in real estate, sports, and entertainment. Donald Trump switched parties where and when it was convenient for his businesses. He didn't care about the ins and outs of the everyday Washington clamor. He donated to campaigns and rubbed elbows with whichever politician could be influenced to do what he wanted. Ladies and gentlemen, that is how politics works and how things get done.

Back in 1988, Trump talked about what he would do if he was president, and he even hinted at the idea on *The Oprah Winfrey Show*—back when they were bosom buddies. This is the year 1988, before many of you were born or were old enough to pay attention to anything of the sort—let alone who Donald Trump was. Fast forward to 2015. Tired of the direction the country was headed in, and of what was going on in the country he loved, he switched parties AGAIN and announced that he was running for president of the United States from Trump Tower in New York. It was at this moment that half of America and the left-wing media that once adored him began to HATE him. This was not a coincidence or some old feud brewing in the closet; this was calculated because the beloved Donald J. Trump (D) was now Donald J. Trump (R)—and was taking his money, contacts, and fame with him to the other side of the aisle.

President Donald J. Trump was sworn in as the forty-fifth president of the United States on January 20, 2016. Beating out a crowded field of Republicans and Democrats. Most of them, by most political metrics, out-qualified him for the job. But why Trump? The brash New Yorker who didn't care about your feelings, who said whatever formulated in his mind and transmitted to his lips, was exactly what resonated with millions of Americans from every stripe who voted for him, and with millions of foreigners around the world who adored him. The media never saw anything like it, so they had to become the villain—as did many politicians, bureaucrats, and YOU, the everyday citizen who got convinced to hate Trump. Everything from rape allegations, Russian collusion, impeachments over phone calls and orchestrated riots, and the "bad" handling of the plandemic—that is right, PLANDEMIC. It was planned. I think you have gotten the memo by now. And how can we forget January 6? But this was all Trump's fault, and he and solely he was to blame and must pay the price of being removed from office—though Hillary says he rigged and stole the election from her, but anyways....

In 2020, you elected Joe R. Biden. Many have since crawled into a corner and cried and kicked themselves in the rear end for such a decision. But nonetheless, here we are. He's pushing an agenda along with the rest of the Democratic Party that no one is cheering for—not from the constituency anyways. Gas prices are up. Inflation through the roof. Russia invaded Ukraine. The Afghanistan withdrawal was a disaster resulting in thirteen service members killed. Border crisis. Illegal immigration is out of control. Foreign leaders laughing and making fun of Biden. They did it to Trump, too, but at least he made them respect him and did what he said. Corruption with his son, Hunter Biden—that was suppressed and still is. Our domestic policies and foreign policies are in shambles. People think this is okay versus what we had under Trump. Trump created a sixth branch in the military, the Space Force. Fixed the Flint water crisis. Signed two laws to combat human/sex trafficking. Created Opportunity Zones in low income and poverty-stricken communities. Stabilized and normalized relations in middle-eastern countries. The US surpassed Russia and Saudi Arabia in oil production, leading to energy independence. The list literally goes on and on. If Americans want to enjoy a truly free and prosperous nation again, then Trump would be the one to get the job done, based on his past performance. But if being mean and firing mediocre people and attacking the media is not your flavor, then vote for the other person and then cry in the corner with regret in 2025.

The Great Enchanter—Barack Obama April 2024

In 2007, a relatively unknown senator from Illinois by the name of Barack Hussein Obama entered the public spotlight by running for president of the United States. His charisma, his young looks, his family, and arguably his mannerisms and articulation made him a very attractive and ideal person for the presidency. There were one—well—a couple of big problems. Barack Obama had to make America identify with him. His handlers made sure to bury his community organizing days, since such works were generally linked with socialist provocateur Saul Alinsky from the ’60s and ’70s. They also had to move perception of him beyond being the child of a biracial couple who was then raised by a white family in Hawaii. How can he truly identify with Black America? That wasn’t important—nor was it really the impending question. The question was, can he appeal to white America enough but look Black enough to win over the Black vote? The answer was astounding: YES, HE CAN!

The Obama campaign understood this dynamic very well. He had to appeal to White America—never mind Black America. Black America was happy enough to see a man who appeared so Black running for president. That was good enough and garnered their vote hook, line, and sinker! White America needed a little more. They needed some assurance that he wasn’t going to play the “vote for me because I’m Black, and if you don’t, you’re racist" card. So, Obama brought substance and valid talking points that Americans by and large wanted to hear from a presidential candidate. I spoke to many Obama enthusiasts during the 2007 campaign cycle and found that many didn't care what he had to say or what he was about. He was Black. He had a (D) next to his name. And his family was Black. Check. Check. Check. Some Black Americans weren't buying it, however. You mean to tell me that a Black man coming from a mostly white family is going to walk into the White House with no strings attached? Now there's a thought most people, including me, didn't think about. How is it that a Black man will become the nation's first Black president with virtually no pushback in 2008? Did we really come that far? Did change really happen that we could believe in? NOPE.

Was America ready to elect Hillary Rodham Clinton, the wife of former President Bill Clinton? No. Not because she was a woman, but because she was Bill Clinton's wife. It reeked of nepotism and corruption, and Americans weren't really ready to grapple with it. That is largely why Bill stayed out of the picture for most of her campaign run. Did we want to see Senator John McCain as president? A decorated war hero and former prisoner of war, yet a moment's notice away from handing the reins over to former Alaska Governor Sarah Palin? This was another NOPE. This is where the "lesser of two evils" idea comes in. Barack checked nearly all the boxes for Americans. We could stomach him for four years and see what would happen. Black America just knew they were getting reparations! Black America turned out overwhelmingly for Barack in 2008. On election night, chants in Grant Park in Chicago were heard: "We put him in the White House!" "We got him elected!" Now what?

A lot of Black Americans felt disillusioned with the Obama presidency. The commonly themed "Black issues" in America were not addressed, fixed, or even offered solutions by Democrats after the 2008 election, and definitely not during the 2012 through 2016 years. White Americans saw Obama as an opportunist in stoking racial tensions. Obama interjected himself in nearly every controversial matter surrounding violence toward African Americans from cops. He often remarked about the newly created buzzword "systemic racism." Yet he was elected by this very same system. Of course, this was a talking point to appease the far-left crowd that espoused this rhetoric. His presidency reflected the typical establishment politics, with favoritism toward the LBGTQ+ agenda. This is what mostly made Black America upset with former President Obama. He sold lip service to the Black community while committing full-on service through the stroke of the pen to ALL other communities. While he tried to portray the ideal role that Americans envisioned of a president, at the end of the day, President Barack Obama was par for the course.

Mike Pence and the Bedfellows

I will preface this article with one fact. The DOJ dropped the investigation into former Vice President Mike Pence's possession of classified documents. I'll let you ruminate on that as I begin. It isn't a surprise in Republican circles that Mike Pence threw his hat into the ring to run for president of the United States; after all, it is the next logical step in his political career path. Pence, however, isn't likely to get very far even with the help of his Democratic colleagues. He is a man of principle. High moral standards. A code of honor that isn't seen among politicians since the days of Lincoln—also known as Honest Abe. But is Pence really a principled and moral man? Sure, he won't meet with another woman outside the presence of his wife. I think no man would, if he has a known weakness for women and wants to avoid putting himself in position for being #MeTooed. But can a politician be as seemingly straight as Pence? Of course not! This is why he will make the PERFECT president.

Pence running against Trump isn't out of some idea that he really wants to challenge the man because he feels he can do a better job. No. This is out of spite toward Trump for having done a very good job! Trump gave Pence the limelight when he needed to, but not because Pence was doing something extraordinary as vice president to deserve national attention. Being put in charge of the Coronavirus Task Force was his "knight in shining armor" moment as VP, and we all can see how that went. Trump was right back in the spotlight a few weeks later. While Pence's leadership may be remarkable in some areas, his impudence and indecisiveness on many issues is where he appears weak to the lurking wolves. This is why there are many Democrats who LOVE him. They know that if they dangle the Bible in front of him and say "turn the other cheek," he will cave in to their demands. If he's elected president—and that is a big IF—who would be his VP? My choice in the matter would be Governor Ron DeSantis. The second option is former Governor Chris Christie. DeSantis and Christie have a love-hate relationship with Trump. Whoever Pence's pick will be—though it may not specifically be *his* pick—will need to be part of the establishment politics of Washington.

Well, what about Nikki Haley, Tim Scott, and Vivek Ramaswamy, or Larry Elder? Nikki will have a role in the cabinet as secretary of state. Senator Tim Scott may be well suited to head the HUD or even the Treasury. These are all bedfellows within the Republican Party establishment circles. Vivek Ramaswamy and Larry Elder won't be considered for anything. They are Trump allies. Their messaging is closely aligned with that of Trump, and if there is any inkling of Trump's influence permeating the Pence campaign/cabinet, it will be sought out and exterminated with brute force. The old saying that the GOP and the Democrats are two wings of the same bird is very true. But in order to take that bird off its course, you need to pluck its feathers, clip its wings, and clip its claws. My preferred method is Alka-Seltzer—and get the nonsense over with. But we can't be doing that; we need the bird. We just need the bird grounded into reality—so that they can listen to the people and not to their own egos soaring in the sky of illusions at our expense.

For Pence, should he see it through to the end and clinch the nomination, the one person in the current field who he needs at his side to keep the wolves off his back would be Trump or Elder. DeSantis would be a possible option, but I am afraid he has too much respect for his elders to really go after them as they may need. I stopped mentioning Chris Christie because he doesn't hold the sway needed with either side, let alone within the party, to really have the desired impact. Pence is the ace in the hole that both the Republicans and Democrats are hoping will clinch the nomination. You know why? See my opening.

Juneteenth: A Peculiar Holiday

Legend has it that in the spring of 1863, a few months after the issuance of the Emancipation Proclamation that freed the slaves in the rebelling Confederate states, a group of Black Union soldiers from Louisiana who were on a scouting mission in southern Texas came across a plantation where slaves were still working. One of the soldiers belted out from a distance, "Hey, y'alls are free now! Gone outta here!" The few slaves that heard him said he was lying and a fool for trying to get them to run away and continued to work. He was bewildered at the response and rode off to catch up with his colleagues and didn't mention the encounter to the other soldiers. A similar account of this situation was captured in the movie *Emancipation*, starring Will Smith. Whether this is true or not, I am inclined to believe there is some validity to this story. After all, how is it that one area of Texas didn't get the "memo" that the rest of the nation got? That had to be the best-kept secret until the US government's recent revelation and admission about UFOs.

I will further posit that when a Black person tells a group of Black people something that is for their own benefit and goes against the grain of their own groupthink ideologies, they are met with skepticism and most often ridicule; so once again, I don't doubt the validity here. Well, fast-forwarding two years later, it took a white general by the name of Gordon Granger and his troops to issue General Order No. 3, which declared—and reinforced—that the slaves were, in fact, free. Celebrations of freedom rang out in the streets of Galveston, Texas. Some slaves didn't know what to make of their newfound freedom, some stayed on the plantation and worked for wages—this system later became known as sharecropping in the south. All the while, from 1863 to much of 1865, the Civil War was still raging. Slaves were continuously being liberated from plantations and prisons. States that were still part of the Union and did not secede—Kentucky, Delaware, Maryland, and Missouri—were allowed to keep their slaves. Only the ratification of the Thirteenth Amendment on December 6, 1865, freed all slaves in the United States.

Those in favor of making Juneteenth a federal holiday make the justification that it marks the freedom of the last of the slaves still in bondage. Well, this isn't the case. To be more specific, although the Thirteenth Amendment abolished slavery in 1865, the Choctaw

Nation didn't free their slaves until the Reconstruction Treaty of 1866. While many Cherokee slave owners ignored the law during this period, the governing body of the Cherokee Nation signed a treaty on July 27, 1866, assigning all freed slaves and their descendants the same rights as those of the native Cherokees. This is what we call cherry-picking history to fit, or build, a narrative of sorts. Juneteenth was chosen not so much for historical accuracy of ALL slaves being freed, but for some in an area that didn't get the memo for one reason or another. Now, you may ask, should we not celebrate Juneteenth? Yes, we can. Yes, you can. Yes, it should be a celebration. Perhaps more suitable for a state holiday instead of a federal one. I would propose making December 6 the actual federal holiday signifying the freedom of Blacks in America due to the abolition of slavery. If we are going to make an argument of inclusivity for freedom from slavery, then it should be the date the government abolished it. Black America was pacified with this holiday as a reward for delivering the votes for President Biden. Now the Black community is saddled with a holiday that celebrates a few thousand slaves who didn't know they were already free, while at least four other states and a couple of native tribes still practiced slavery. Well played, Democrats. Well played... Next up on the deck is faking reparations. See my previous article about that one.

Gun Control
January 2024

Advocates for gun control can never actually define what gun control means. There is also no consensus on what gun control should look like. This is exactly why we have over five thousand laws on the books—from the municipal to the federal level—surrounding various gun control measures. And here's the news flash: Criminals still don't abide by them, nor do they care about the laws—hence the definition of a criminal as someone who willfully broke the law. Gun control laws, I would argue, would be reasonable to some degree in terms of preventative measures to protect children. These could include safety locks, storage requirements, and even supervised use for anyone under the age of eighteen. That would be literally it when it comes to gun control laws. Those in favor of banning guns or restricting gun ownership have not found themselves in a position where a gun was useful or where they needed to defend themselves or others. They are typically from a demographic that is generally insulated from society and will not place themselves in areas that have a propensity for violence.

The Second Amendment is quite clear. I'll spare you the details, but the phrase "the right to keep and bear arms SHALL NOT BE INFRINGED" seems to always get overlooked when the topic of gun control comes up—especially in conversations about banning "assault weapons" and/or "red-flag" laws. If you read the Bill of Rights, you will notice that no other right is enshrined with the words "shall not be infringed." The framers of the Constitution understood how critical the fundamental right to self-preservation, self-protection, and the protection of property, and those who may be defenseless, was to preserving this Republic not only from its own government but also from foreign invaders and fringe elements within society. Foreign aggressions and even large-scaled attacks are rare. It isn't because of technology or the lack of will to fight; it's because everyone understands that there is a whole population that is potentially armed to the teeth and will kill anyone who tries to invade.

I am a gun owner and gun carrier. I am trained and licensed. I've served this nation for over twenty-two years in the United States Army and been on three combat tours in Iraq and a contingency operation tour in Kuwait. I have lived in Europe and traveled around various European countries and Canada. What I have found in all these locations is that citizens live relatively peaceful lives, and when violence strikes, it is by way of vehicles, knives, bats, and bombs. On a few occasions, guns are involved. Have you heard about banning or controlling cars, knives, bats, or bombs? Why is that? I'll tell you why—because these items are recognized as essential tools of society for whatever reason and their nefarious use is blamed on the person, not the tool. The very same argument can and should be made for guns. Guns are simply a tool. In Iraq, our fear was roadside bombs, known as improvised explosive devices (IEDs). They could be found stuffed in dead cows lying in the road, in potholes, and even embedded into the road by highly skilled construction crews. We weren't too concerned about gunfire. Imagine if IEDs became a concern in the US because guns became unavailable or restricted. I'll take you back to Oklahoma City, 1995. Timothy McVeigh and Terry Nichols loaded a moving truck full of fertilizer and parked it in a parking garage of the Alfred P. Murrah Federal Building, and killed dozens. Then, on September 11, 2001, hijackers flew airplanes into buildings, killing thousands. Where is the conversation on banning trucks, fertilizer, and planes—or even buildings for that matter?

It is hypocritical and nonsensical to want to target a tool for drastic control measures and punish the law-abiding because of the lawless. It is asinine to advertise gun-free zones and tell someone they can't carry a gun because it may scare others. Gun laws that are restrictive or of a banning nature are emphatically and categorically unconstitutional. If we are so concerned for the safety of children or others, then I welcome the conversation to control or ban every tool out there that can potentially be used in mass murder. Until then, spare me the fake outrage.

Blacks Fall for the Reparations Gimmick Again
June 2024

Anyone in the world is for free money, where and when warranted. However, when it comes down to the reparations for Black Americans, I tend to bat an eye and disagree on the principle of it all. Every election cycle, it seems that reparations become a topic and appear on some Democrat's agenda. The basis—generally speaking—is that during slavery and for many years post-slavery, Black Americans were not able to gain the generational wealth seen today among other ethnic groups. While this is a fair argument, given the complicated historical background and circumstances of the late 1800s and the Reconstruction Era, it is quite impossible to just say, "If you're Black in America, then you get a check!" Believe it or not, not ALL Blacks in America today can claim slavery affiliation from nearly two hundred years ago. Some Blacks today will find that their very own ancestors, who were Black, owned slaves themselves. What about the Blacks who were freed and given land, money, and even businesses, but squandered it off or fell victim to capitalism?

If my great-great-great-grandparents owned land and passed it down through the generations, but my grandparents sold it for some selfish reason, got suckered into a bad deal, or simply blew the proceeds without leaving anything for their children and grandchildren, do WE have the right to demand a do-over just because we were not beneficiaries of a sanctioned enterprise from centuries before? What do we say or do about the current market of slavery in the form of human trafficking and sex trafficking going on in the US and even in the African countries of our ancestry? Some of our relatives may be current victims of modern-day slavery, but we are mum on the situation because "it's not us!" Many Black people today cannot trace their lineage further than their great grandparents—who, by the way, were likely not slaves—so what metrics or standards should be applied to Black Americans today to qualify them for a "reparations package"? Oh, by the way, since we are in the era of IDENTIFYING as whatever we want, EVERY PERSON in the United States will identify as Black. After all, Black people started humanity out of Africa, right? Will the "one-drop rule" apply to paying out reparations?

Let's just say that proving genetic lineage to enslaved ancestors was the only criterion to qualify for this "payment." What would the amount be? Where would it come from? Would it be one time, quarterly, annually? What would stop subsequent generations from demanding reparations once this issue is "paid in full"? Hence, we are having this discussion again post-Reconstruction. Can African Americans deal with the consequences and repercussions of the social ills and resentment from other Blacks and ethnic groups that didn't get a penny, or the equivalent thereof? Understand the difference between African American and Black, and there is a difference. To my fellow African Americans and Black people, stop falling for the gimmick that some politician, organization, or BS commission tells you that you are owed reparations and you will get it. The only thing that will come from it is that you will run to the nearest polling booth and check their name, and they will smile at the idea of fooling you—whether in their sleep or on their way to the nearest bank to cash that check from the nonprofit they created in the name of fighting for reparations for

"Black people." Accept the fact that we are in a time and space where we must work, save, and build for ourselves and our posterity, because it won't be given to us for free or in any form of retroactive payment for work YOU NEVER DID for folks you never worked for.

Black Christians' Cognitive Dissonance May 2024

There's a growing conversation within the Black community church leaders surrounding the lack of faith and lack of religion among our youth and even the middle-aged groups of thirty- to fifty-year-olds. Among these groups, church attendance, or a declared religious affiliation, has dropped. A Pew Research Center report from May 2023 shows that Black Protestant churches have witnessed a 15 percent drop in attendance in the post-COVID era. While 47 percent of a sample size of 3,394 say they attend church at least once a week, they remain the highest among nearly all ethnic groups to do so—but still low given the historical trend of being the largest minority religious group in America. There is a burning question as to why Black America is losing its religion. But more importantly, will Black churches do what is required to change the downward trajectory?

The increased use of social media and the growth of social justice organizations have placed the Kumbaya church on the back-burner. The vast majority of pastors across the country have bent the Bible and the words of Christ to fit the narratives of today's politics and pop-culture trends to appease the crowds and to appease the government from coming down on them and threatening their 501(c)(3) status. This sort of acquiescing to the masses has turned off those who are looking for shepherds of the flock who are unafraid of speaking the truth and standing by the word of God versus bending and omitting things to avoid being controversial. Black faith leaders are afraid to speak out against abortion, homosexuality, and transgenderism; they are afraid to express their TRUE political views because they know that their congregations are generational Democrat voters—most of the pastors are as well. This brings us to this conundrum or enigma within the Black Christian population and their failure to recognize the damage it has caused.

The generational devotion to the Democratic Party by the Black community, as demonstrated by a 90+ percent voting rate coupled with their religious affiliation, leaves non-Black religious people scratching their heads as to why the Black community is so beholden to the Democratic Party, which does not align with its religious values? These are the facts in comparison with every other ethnic group and their religious affiliations. In my recent interview with Vincent E. Ellison, he made a strong point about why the Black community is committed to the Democratic Party—Dr. Rev. Martin Luther King Jr.! He highlighted many points about this conundrum in his documentary *Will You Go to Hell for Me?* Aside from that, I, too, have asked the question and wonder why I am met with such vitriol for the inquiry and the defense of my position as a conservative. When we look at the predominantly Black-occupied communities/cities around the country, coupled with nearly seventy years of Democratic Party rule in every one of them, it is no wonder why many Blacks are moving out and into more diverse neighborhoods.

Blacks who have a religious affiliation or who have declared a faith but not a specific church have become increasingly inclined toward attending a diverse church versus an all-Black church due to much of the internal rhetoric that transpires—the groupthink mentality. These same Blacks are the ones who are embracing their TRUE identity as conservatives. While some will still not openly admit it due to the potential backlash from friends and family, you can tell who they are just by their lifestyle and the way they carry themselves. Many get the idea of being conservative wrong. It is not solely a political ideology—it is a lifestyle. It is what keeps liberals in business. Without conservatives, liberalism would die where it stands. It is much like socialism: It is great being a liberal until you run out of other people's money. Being conservative is understanding the principles of Maslow's hierarchy of needs. Being conservative means being grounded in your belief systems and standing up for those beliefs—not changing course because a new trend is out or because some TikTok influencer says so.

It's time for the Black faith leaders to reclaim their communities and live up to the values and principles that they were ordained to live by. Stop being afraid of the groupthink crowds, stop being afraid of the government, stop being afraid of being uncomfortable. Jesus wasn't comfortable when he died on the cross—neither should you be comfortable, dying to spread the gospel in his name and saving souls—not helping to condemn them.

Affirmative Action in College Admissions: Why It Doesn't Matter! October 2024

How many people do you know who have been denied college admissions based on their race? Better yet, how many people do you know who desire to go to college these days? Many people who aspire for higher education will get it regardless of what barriers they may presumably or possibly face. They may not go to Harvard or Yale, but they will opt to go to an online school or another university that may have lower barriers of entry. Skin color, ethnicity, or race—whatever you want to place the label on—doesn't matter when seeking an endeavor of excellence. You will either succeed or you won't. You will try harder or give up.

Minorities who seek affirmative action programs and policies should actually pause and think for a second: These programs send the message that their placement isn't based on their merits, test scores, or prior academic achievements, but rather on a preconceived idea that they are inherently inferior and need the bar lowered to be in the company of their peers. That is essentially what affirmative action has become in recent years. It isn't so much about meeting quotas to achieve diversification with merit still in mind, but more about appeasing the "everyone gets a trophy" mob.

When we look at educational attainment in the United States by ethnicity, the numbers are relatively proportionate for each group. In other words, not everyone will go to college, and not everyone will succeed in school. So, is affirmative action necessary when natural attrition will run its course anyway?

Besides, most of these universities have gone mad-liberal left and are not really yielding the thought leaders of tomorrow anyways. Most people recognize this and opt to attend trade school or look back in hindsight and realize they didn't learn much of anything in their degree field but are stuck with hefty student loan debt that's been promised to be forgiven but hasn't been yet. Sorry to say it, but gender studies or race relations in the twenty-first century won't yield a six-figure income—ANYWHERE.

Let's think about this for a second: The five-year graduation rates in bachelor's programs are 62.2 percent for White or Caucasian students, 41.5 percent for Hispanic or Latino students,

40.5 percent for Black or African American students, and 69.3 percent for Asian/Pacific Islander students.[150] We can speculate as to why these numbers are what they are, but what it tells me is that based on population density per group, each group demonstrates ethics of study and work according to what is reflected in society overall.

Should these groups be punished because of their respective success rates? When was the last time you called off work to "BS" around or simply because you didn't want to go? As I love to say, we are a product of our decisions, not our circumstances. Sure, access to resources may be a factor, but it's also not an excuse for lower attainment in some groups compared to others. Two members of the SCOTUS demonstrated that through their opposing opinions: Justices Brown Jackson and Thomas. We all can agree that they are qualified authorities on the matter. We can also qualify the authority on the matter on the basis of our own children's behavior and attitude toward school. No other person knows their child better than the parent, and this Supreme Court decision sealed the fate for you—you now know whether your child will have a chance at furthering their academic future on the basis of their skills, not so much their skin color. Some of you were hoping for the latter, and you know I am not lying.

If we want to solve this problem, then we must simply eliminate these identifying demographic questions from the applications/admissions process. But we won't do that because we need a mechanism in place to fall back on when it's time to cry about something that didn't go our way. Also, it would be antithetical

150 Imed Bouchrika, "Number of College Graduates: 2025 Race, Gender, Age & State Statistics," Research.com, September 19, 2025, https://research.com/universities-colleges/number-of-college-graduates#3.

to the DEI movement and special-interest groups that track these things for a living. Circle of Life 101....

The future of America will be fine in this regard. It just forced college-aspiring people to really examine themselves among their peers and make themselves as competitive as possible. But at the same time, it will motivate these schools to devise new methods to discriminate and gather their flock as they see fit—as they already do and as they always have. In other words, nothing changes.

REFERENCES

INTRODUCTION

The Great Switch: How the Democrats and Republicans Flipped Ideologies. Students of History. 2023. https://www.studentsofhistory.com/ideologies-flip-Democratic-Republican-parties

US Congress. 2023. Commission to Study Reparations. https://www.congress.gov/bill/118th-congress/senate-bill/40?q=%7B%22search%22%3A%22Commission+to+study+reparations%22%7D&s=2&r=1

US Congress. 2023. Inflation Reduction Act. Congress.gov. https://www.congress.gov/bill/118th-congress/house-bill/812?q=%7B%22search%22%3A%22Inflation+Reduction+Act%22%7D&s=1&r=2

NRDC. 2022. What is the Keystone Pipeline. Denchak, Melissa, Lindwall, Courtney. https://www.nrdc.org/stories/what-keystone-xl-pipeline#whatis

Benjamin, Frank. 2016. You Know You're a Republican...Democrat If...Sourcebooks.

CH.1

The Commonwealth Fund. 2025. The Effects of Eliminating the Individual Mandate Penalty and the Role of Bad Behaviors. https://

www.commonwealthfund.org/publications/fund-reports/2018/jul/eliminating-individual-mandate-penalty-behavioral-factors

US Census Bureau. 2024. Population: Quick Facts. https://www.census.gov/quickfacts/fact/table/US/RHI225223

US Supreme Court. 2019. No.18–1171—ComCast Corporation v. National Association of African-American Owned Media, et. al. https://www.supremecourt.gov/DocketPDF/18/18-1171/116542/20190920143641893_18-1171%20Amicus%20Brief%20of%20ISSUES4LIFE%20Foundation.pdf

California Senate Republicans. 2019. California Democrats Protect Offenders Who Lure Minors. https://src.senate.ca.gov/content/california-democrats-protect-offenders-who-lure-minors

Farmer, Ryan. 2022. 2022 House Bill 209: Maryland Democrats Seek to Legalize Acts of Bestiality. The News and Times. https://www.newsandtimes.com/politics/2022/01/2022-house-bill-209-maryland-democrats-seek-to-legalize-acts-of-bestiality/

Library of Congress. 1802. Jefferson's Letter to the Danbury Baptists: Final Letter as Sent. https://www.loc.gov/loc/lcib/9806/danpre.html

Chishti, Muzaffar & Bolter, Jessica. 2019. Remain in Mexico Plan Echoes Earlier U.S. Policy to Deter Haitian Migration. Migration Policy Institute. https://www.migrationpolicy.org/article/remain-mexico-plan-echoes-earlier-us-policy-deter-haitian-migration

Common Core Standards States Initiative. 2012. https://web.archive.org/web/20140226221237/http://www.corestandards.org/resources/frequently-asked-questions

US Congress. 2017. PUBLIC LAW 115–97—DEC. 22, 2017. https://www.congress.gov/bill/115th-congress/house-bill/1/text

CH. 2

Fox News. 2016. BIAS ALERT: Did NBC Sit on Trump Hot Mic Footage?. https://www.foxnews.com/politics/bias-alert-did-nbc-sit-on-trump-hot-mic-footage

LA Times. 2017. Read the complete transcript of President Trump's remarks at Trump Tower on Charlottesville. https://www.latimes.com/politics/la-na-pol-trump-charlottesville-transcript-20170815-story.html

CNN Business. 2020. Newsmax and OANN are telling lies about the election as more people tune in. https://www.cnn.com/videos/business/2020/11/23/newsmax-oan-trump-conspiracy-theories-ratings-orig-vf.cnnbusiness

New York Post. 2021. Marsh, Julie, Kennedy, Dana, and Linge, Mary Kay. Chris Cuomo fired from CNN over involvement with brother Andrew's scandals. https://nypost.com/2021/12/04/chris-cuomo-fired-from-cnn-over-involvement-with-brother-andrews-scandals/

The Independent. 2025. Baragona, Justin. Joy Reid's final show: Fired MSNBC host leaves viewers with dire message after controversial axing. https://www.the-independent.com/news/world/americas/us-politics/joy-reid-final-show-fascism-b2704385.htm

Rocky Mountain Outlook. 2022. Bauder, David. Rachel Maddow returns to MSNBC, will switch to once a week. https://www.

rmoutlook.com/lifestyle/rachel-maddow-returns-to-msnbc-will-switch-to-once-a-week-5256313

National Review. 2024. The Editors. Biden's Social-Media Censorship Regime.https://www.nationalreview.com/2024/08/bidens-social-media-censorship-regime/

House Judiciary Committee. 2023. Press Release. Testimony Reveals FBI Employees Who Warned Social Media Companies about Hack and Leak Operation Knew Hunter Biden Laptop Wasn't Russian Disinformation. https://judiciary.house.gov/media/press-releases/testimony-reveals-fbi-employees-who-warned-social-media-companies-about-hack

Associated Press. 2021. Bauder, David. Two Fox News political executives out after Arizona call. https://apnews.com/article/joe-biden-donald-trump-arizona-elections-a11f8112a58eb458 54be59f64d47e1dc

Election Night Channel. 2020. When Fox News called Arizona for Joe Biden (Election 2020). YouTube.https://www.youtube.com/watch?v=wrDYcS9qskE

The Hill. 2022. Cochran, Lexi Lonas. DirecTV declines to renew OAN contract. https://thehill.com/homenews/media/589871-directv-declines-to-renew-one-america-news-networks-contract/

CBC. 2022. Brend, Yvette. Celebs like Tom Brady, Larry David did ads for crypto giant FTX. Now they're getting sued. https://www.cbc.ca/news/business/bankruptcy-class-action-ftx-cryptocurrency-bailout-bankman-fried-1.6655836

Lioness of Judah Ministry. 2025. Safe and Effective: 2,000 Hollywood Celebrities, European Elite Caught with Fake

Vaccination Passports. https://lionessofjudah.substack.com/p/safe-and-effective-2000-hollywood?utm_campaign=post&utm_medium=web

CH. 3

Voice of America. 2020. Farivar, Massod. Anarchist Groups Tied to Riots in 4 US Cities. Extremist Watch. https://www.voanews.com/a/extremism-watch_anarchist-groups-tied-riots-4-us-cities/6195936.html

The Christian Post. 2020. Brown, Michael. The mayor of Seattle has a rude awakening about CHOP. https://www.christianpost.com/voices/the-mayor-of-seattle-has-a-rude-awakening-about-chop.html

New York Post. 2022. Vincent, Isabel. BLM spent at least $12M on luxury properties in LA, Toronto: tax filing. https://nypost.com/2022/05/17/black-lives-matter-spent-at-least-12-million-on-mansions/

Fox Baltimore News. 2020. Baron, Julian. Black Lives Matter faces growing rift with local chapters over finances and transparency. https://foxbaltimore.com/news/nation-world/black-lives-matter-faces-rift-with-local-chapters-over-finances

ABC 7 News Bay Area. 2020. Trump Rally turns violent in Sacramento as Proud Boys, Antifa face off. https://www.youtube.com/watch?v=I7yHxW6eIqI

Discovery Institute. 2021. Myers, Walter III. Critical Race Theory—The Marxist Trojan Horse. In Indoctrination. The

Bottom Line. https://www.discovery.org/education/2021/08/05/critical-race-theory-the-marxist-trojan-horse/

Alliance Defending Freedom. 2021. Hardin, Neal. What Is Critical Race Theory? https://adflegal.org/article/what-critical-race-theory/

Defending Education. 2021. Press Release. Full NSBA Letter to Biden Administration and Department of Justice Memo. https://defendinged.org/press-releases/full-nsba-letter-to-biden-administration-and-department-of-justice-memo/

Daily Citizen. 2021. Johnston, Jeff. State School Board Associations Separating from National School Boards Association. https://dailycitizen.focusonthefamily.com/state-school-board-associations-separating-from-national-school-boards-association/

New York Times Magazine. 2019. The 1619 Project—Inter-active. https://www.nytimes.com/interactive/2019/08/14/magazine/1619-america-slavery.html

Legal Defense Fund. 2021. Nikole Hannah-Jones Issues Statement on Decision to Decline Tenure Offer at University of North Carolina-Chapel Hill and to Accept Knight Chair Appointment at Howard University. https://www.naacpldf.org/press-release/nikole-hannah-jones-issues-statement-on-decision-to-decline-tenure-offer-at-university-of-north-carolina-chapel-hill-and-to-accept-knight-chair-appointment-at-howard-university/

Legal Defense Fund. 2022. Nikole Hannah-Jones Reaches Settlement Agreement with the University of North Carolina at Chapel Hill. https://www.naacpldf.org/press-release/nikole-hannah-jones-reaches-settlement-agreement-with-the-university-of-north-carolina-at-chapel-hill/

CASEL. 2023. What is SEL? https://casel.org/fundamentals-of-sel/what-is-the-casel-framework/#:~:text=Self%2Dawareness:%20The%20abilities%20to,sense%20of%20confidence%20and%20purpose.

YouTube. 2022. Rocky IV Scene. https://www.youtube.com/watch?v=WvAeWtyZ-uE

The Guardian. 2021. Reed. Betsy. Let children play': the educational message from across Europe. https://www.theguardian.com/society/2021/apr/23/let-children-play-the-educational-message-from-across-europe.

CH. 4

Medium. 2022. Harrell, Gary C. Ruby Bridges, Cancel Culture & the Denial of American History. https://gcharrell1975.medium.com/ruby-bridges-cancel-culture-the-denial-of-american-history-a0ccc3d0902b

Newsweek. 2020. Bond, Paul. Meet the Young, Black Conservatives Who Are Stumping for Trump—Despite the Backlash. https://www.newsweek.com/meet-young-black-conservatives-who-are-stumping-trumpdespite-backlash-1538815

Hoover Institute. 1999. Steele, Shelby. The Loneliness of the "Black Conservative." https://www.hoover.org/research/loneliness-black-conservative

National Institute of Health. National Library of Medicine. 2024. Am J Public Health. The Hispanic/Latino Population in the United States: Our Black Identity, Our Health and Well-Being. DOI: 10.2105/AJPH.2024.307682. https://pmc.ncbi.nlm.nih.gov/articles/PMC11292280/#:~:text=The%20Hispanic/Latino%20population%20represents,by%202050%20(128%20million).

Intellectual Takeout. Miltimore, Jon. 2016. Did LBJ Say, 'I'll have those n*ggers voting Democratic for 200 years'?. https://intellectualtakeout.org/2016/10/did-lbj-say-ill-have-those-nggers-voting-democratic-for-200-years/

Goodreads. 2025. Lyndon Baines Johnson. Quotes. Quotable Quotes. https://www.goodreads.com/quotes/7107768-these-negroes-they-re-getting-pretty-uppity-these-days-and-that-s

CH. 5

Participedia. 2014. All Lives Matter. Creative Common. Case. https://participedia.net/case/5563?lang=en

The Diamondback. 2020. Rosenberg, Maya. White people need to be listening to black activists, not talking over them. https://dbknews.com/2020/06/06/george-floyd-protests-racism-black-lives-matter/

Truthout. 2015. Crass, Chris. For White Anti-Racists Holding Back From Stepping Up in These Black Lives Matter Movement Times. https://truthout.org/articles/for-white-anti-racists-holding-back-from-stepping-up-in-these-black-lives-matter-movement-times/

The Independent. 2021. Bremner, Jake. Coca-Cola faces backlash over seminar asking staff to 'be less white'. https://www.the-independent.com/life-style/coca-cola-racism-robin-diangelo-coke-b1806122.html

Yahoo News. 2023. Blaff, Ari. Robin DiAngelo Advises People of Color to 'Get Away from White People'. National Review. https://www.yahoo.com/news/robin-diangelo-advises-people-color-195511417.html?guccounter=1&guce_referrer=aHR0cHM6Ly93d3cuZ29vZ2xlLmNvbS8&guce_referrer_sig=AQAAANOYomANOeLaLbpWvTD8y0fYOg3b8q1oWuFM77A7ATOVoe5snkQvSLtBb-cVHg0b8tw1ktmVDI8LOxK0wU8h-bzuOmsz0U93hzMXThpS8SIjUzC60cSWeorg8Wco1ojTrhFN3dUA-nTKSM4PQgOeMlViKOWKk4qy-6p6_bA99fbi

Black Agenda Report. 2020. Ford, Glen. BLM Chapters Demand "Accountability" from Trio that Cashed in on the Movement. https://www.blackagendareport.com/blm-chapters-demand-accountability-trio-cashed-movement

Daily Mail. 2021. Court, Andrew & Alexander, Harriet. 'How much of her money is actually going to charitable causes?' Head of NYC BLM chapter calls for probe into organization's co-founder as it's revealed 'she has spent $3MILLION on FOUR luxury homes'. https://www.dailymail.co.uk/news/article-9458259/Head-NYCs-BLM-chapter-calls-probe-founder-purchased-expensive-homes.html

Ibid.

YouTube. 1993. Tombstone. Doc Holiday Scene. "My hypocrisy knows no bounds." https://www.youtube.com/watch?v=BdFP0d9wKxA

CH. 6

Your Dictionary. Tomgirl. https://www.yourdictionary.com/tomgirl

Your Dictionary. Tomboy. https://www.yourdictionary.com/tomboy

Bible Gateway. Deuteronomy 22:5. King James Version https://www.biblegateway.com/passage/?search=Deuteronomy%2022%3A5&version=KJV

Bible Gateway. Matthew 5:44. King James Version. https://www.biblegateway.com/passage/?search=Matthew%205%3A44&version=NKJV

Bible Gateway. John 14:15–31. King James Version. https://www.biblegateway.com/passage/?search=John%2014%3A15-31&version=KJV

Bible Gateway. Matthew 7: 9–29. https://www.biblegateway.com/passage/?search=Matthew%207&version=KJV

New York Post. Ruiz, Michael. 2023. Nashville school shooter Audrey Hale had handwritten notes on clothes, numbered anklet: autopsy. https://nypost.com/2023/07/26/nashville-school-shooter-audrey-hale-had-handwritten-notes-on-clothes-numbered-anklet-autopsy/

National Library of Medicine. 2021. Gender affirming medical care of transgender youth. https://pmc.ncbi.nlm.nih.gov/articles/PMC8496167/

Politico. 2022. Ward, Myah. Blackburn to Jackson: Can you define 'the word woman'? https://www.politico.com/news/2022/03/22/blackburn-jackson-define-the-word-woman-00019543

The Advocate: The Student Voice of Contra Costa College. 2017. Santone, Michael. LGBTQ community faces inner conflict. https://cccadvocate.com/7364/opinion/lgbtq-community-faces-inner-conflict/

National Library of Medicine. 2022. Pedophile, Child Lover, or Minor-Attracted Person? Attitudes Toward Labels Among People Who are Sexually Attracted to Children. https://pmc.ncbi.nlm.nih.gov/articles/PMC9663395/

YouTube. 2022. 'Minor Attracted Persons' wanted acceptance from LBGTQ Community. https://www.youtube.com/watch?v=wX-7F4NtO58

YouTube. 2023. Breaking down every letter in 2SLGBTQQIPAA+ | CBC Kids News. https://www.youtube.com/watch?v=4Fn5sKfy-vU

ESPN. 2021. Transgender fighter Alana McLaughlin submits Celine Provost in MMA debut. https://www.espn.com/mma/story/_/id/32186035/transgender-fighter-alana-mclaughlin-submits-celine-provost-mma-debut

Piper, Greg. Virginia school district lets male leer in girls' locker room, use whichever he wants: complaint. https://www.msn.com/en-us/news/us/virginia-school-district-lets-male-leer-in-girls-locker-room-use-whichever-he-wants-complaint/ar-AA1NrnZp?ocid=BingNewsVerp

Cry of the Hawk. 2021. Haigler, Alexis. Trans women vs trans men competing in Olympics. https://cryofthehawk.org/sports/2021/04/27/trans-women-vs-trans-men-competing-in-olympics/

International Olympics Committee. 2024. IOC approves consensus with regard to athletes who have changed sex. https://

www.olympics.com/ioc/news/ioc-approves-consensus-with-regard-to-athletes-who-have-changed-sex-1

CH. 7

Washington Times. 2023. Picket, Kerry. Wray won't say if FBI informants in Capitol riot mob: 'I really need to be careful'. https://www.washingtontimes.com/news/2023/jul/12/christopher-wray-wont-say-if-fbi-informants-capito/

New York Post. 2021. Garger, Kenneth. School board members reportedly targeting parents opposed to critical race theory. https://nypost.com/2021/03/29/school-board-members-reportedly-targeting-parents-opposed-to-critical-race-theory/

New York Post. 2023. Christenson, Josh. House Judiciary report claims 'broken' FBI 'targeting' conservatives. https://nypost.com/2023/05/18/house-judiciary-report-claims-broken-fbi-targeting-conservatives/

Counter Extremism Project. 2023. Jane's Revenge. https://www.counterextremism.com/supremacy/janes-revenge

House Judiciary. 2023. Olohan, Margaret. Republicans to Hold Hearing on DOJ Targeting Pro-Lifers.https://judiciary.house.gov/media/in-the-news/republicans-hold-hearing-doj-targeting-pro-lifers

American Bar Association. 2022. Armed man accused of threatening Kavanaugh is arrested near justice's home. https://www.americanbar.org/advocacy/governmental_legislative_work/publications/washingtonletter/june-22-wl/kavanaugh-0622wl/

YouTube Blog. 2020. Supporting the 2020 Election. https://blog.youtube/news-and-events/supporting-the-2020-us-election/

House Oversight Committee. 2024. The Biden's Influence Peddling Timeline. https://oversight.house.gov/the-bidens-influence-peddling-timeline/

ABC News. 2023. Romero, Laura. Former Twitter execs tell House committee that removal of Hunter Biden laptop story was a 'mistake'. https://abcnews.go.com/US/former-twitter-execs-house-committee-removal-hunter-biden/story?id=96979014

The Washington Post. 2023. Kessler, Glenn. The Hunter Biden laptop and claims of 'Russian disinfo'. https://www.washingtonpost.com/politics/2023/02/13/hunter-biden-laptop-claims-russian-disinfo/

House Judiciary Committee. 2023. Testimony Reveals FBI Employees Who Warned Social Media Companies about Hack and Leak Operation Knew Hunter Biden Laptop Wasn't Russian Disinformation. https://judiciary.house.gov/media/press-releases/testimony-reveals-fbi-employees-who-warned-social-media-companies-about-hack

House Judiciary Committee. 2022. Letter to Parag Agrawal. https://judiciary.house.gov/sites/evo-subsites/republicans-judiciary.house.gov/files/legacy_files/wp-content/uploads/2022/03/2022-03-31-HJC-GOP-to-Twitter-re-Hunter-Biden-story.pdf

The Times of India. 2024. TOI World Desk. Facebook executives suppressed Hunter Biden laptop to gain favor with Biden-Harris administration: Report. https://timesofindia.indiatimes.com/world/us/facebook-executives-suppressed-hunter-biden-laptop-story-to-gain-favor-with-biden-harris-administration-report/articleshow/114784471.cms

Foreign Policy. 2020. Feldwisch-Drentrup. How WHO Became China's Coronavirus Accomplice. https://foreignpolicy.com/2020/04/02/china-coronavirus-who-health-soft-power/

New York Post. 2023. King, Ryan. Fauci roasted as 'fraud' and 'liar' after being confronted with damning study on masks. https://nypost.com/2023/09/03/dr-fauci-gets-roasted-after-being-confronted-with-damning-study-on-masks/

Human Rights Watch. 2021. COVID-19 Triggers Wave of Free Speech Abuse. https://www.hrw.org/news/2021/02/11/covid-19-triggers-wave-free-speech-abuse

Free Speech Center. 2023. Fisher, Deborah. Disinformation Governance Board. https://firstamendment.mtsu.edu/article/disinformation-governance-board/

Newsweek. 2021. Giella, Lauren & McNally, Graham. Fact Check: Did CNN Remove COVID-19 Tracker After Joe Biden Took Office?. https://www.newsweek.com/fact-check-did-cnn-remove-covid-19-tracker-after-joe-biden-took-office-1564233 (This example is to illustrate the example use of the "Death Tracker" not the story itself.)

Washington Examiner. 2021. Shea, Sidney. New Zealand man who died of gunshot wound to be recorded as COVID-19 death: Report. https://www.washingtonexaminer.com/news/638142/new-zealand-man-who-died-of-gunshot-wound-to-be-recorded-as-covid-19-death-report/

Freedom Foundation. 2020. Nelson, Maxford. Washington health officials: Gunshot victims counted as COVID-19 deaths. https://www.freedomfoundation.com/washington/washington-health-officials-gunshot-victims-counted-as-covid-19-deaths/

FactCheck.org. 2020. Fichera, Angelo. Hospital Payments and the COVID-19 Death Count. https://www.factcheck.org/2020/04/hospital-payments-and-the-covid-19-death-count/

Newsweek. 2020. Soo, Kim. Florida Man Killed in Crash Listed as COVID-19 Death, Raising Doubts Over Health Data. https://www.newsweek.com/florida-man-killed-crash-listed-covid-19-death-raising-doubts-over-health-data-1518994

BBC. 2020. Coronavirus: US travel ban on 26 European countries comes into force. https://www.bbc.com/news/world-us-canada-51883728

Our World. 2020. Schwalbe, Nina. We Could Be Vastly Overestimating the Death Rate for COVID-19 — Here's Why. https://ourworld.unu.edu/en/we-could-be-vastly-overestimating-the-death-rate-for-covid-19-heres-why

World Health Organization. 2022. Press Release. 14.9 million excess deaths associated with the COVID-19 pandemic in 2020 and 2021. https://www.who.int/news/item/05-05-2022-14.9-million-excess-deaths-were-associated-with-the-covid-19-pandemic-in-2020-and-2021

CH. 8

Reason. 2020. Soave, Robby. Feminists Who Now Claim They Never Meant 'Believe All Women' Are Gaslighting Us.

https://reason.com/2020/05/19/believe-all-women-me-too-feminists-biden-reade/

The Village Voice. 2013. Hopper, Jessica. Read the "Stomach-Churning" Sexual Assault Accusations Against R. Kelly in Full. https://www.villagevoice.com/read-the-stomach-churning-sexual-assault-accusations-against-r-kelly-in-full/

Forbes. 2020. Borysenko, Karlyn. The Dark Side Of #MeToo: What Happens When Men Are Falsely Accused. https://www.forbes.com/sites/karlynborysenko/2020/02/12/the-dark-side-of-metoo-what-happens-when-men-are-falsely-accused/

Los Angeles Times. 2018. Haberkorn, Jennifer. The GOP wants to know why Feinstein didn't come forward sooner with Kavanaugh allegation.https://www.latimes.com/politics/la-na-pol-congress-kavanaugh-feinstein-20180919-story.html

PBS News. 2018. Barajas, Joshua. See 4 months of Brett Kavanaugh's calendar from 1982. https://www.pbs.org/newshour/politics/see-four-months-of-brett-kavanaughs-calendar-from-1982

USA Today. 2018. Villalobos, Louie. Second woman accuses Brett Kavanaugh of sexual assault in New Yorker report. https://www.usatoday.com/story/news/politics/2018/09/23/brett-kavanaugh-second-woman-accuses-him-sexual-assault-deborah-ramirez/1406607002/

CQ Press. 1991. Clarence Thomas Wins Senate Confirmation. https://library.cqpress.com/cqalmanac/document.php?id=cqal91-1110583

American Rhetoric. 1991. Thomas, Clarence. Statement Before the Senate Judiciary Committee. https://www.americanrhetoric.com/speeches/clarencethomashightechlynching.htm

Feminist Majority Foundation. 2023. Sutanto, Cynthia. Feminism is for men, too. https://feminist.org/news/feminism-is-for-men-too/

CBS News. 2018. Picchi, Aimee. Nike shoes burned, defaced over Colin Kaepernick's "Just Do It" ad. https://www.cbsnews.com/news/colin-kaepernick-nike-ad-just-do-it-shares-ad-boycott/

USA Today. 2018. Peter, Josh. Tim Tebow not happy about 'Tebowing' being brought into national anthem protests debate. https://www.usatoday.com/story/sports/2018/06/08/tim-tebow-kneeling-national-anthem/686533002/

Forbes. 2018. Swan, Andy. The Numbers Behind Papa John's Brand Devastation. https://www.forbes.com/sites/andyswan/2018/07/25/the-numbers-behind-papa-johns-brand-devastation/

Washington Examiner. 2020. Neale, Spencer. Chris Cuomo: 'Show me where it says that protests are supposed to be polite and peaceful'. https://www.washingtonexaminer.com/news/2617103/chris-cuomo-show-me-where-it-says-that-protests-are-supposed-to-be-polite-and-peaceful/

YouTube. 2020. Daily Wire+. The Andrew Klavin Show. CNN's Chris Cuomo DOWNPLAYS Rioting Concerns. https://youtu.be/oxo5DjCyKq8?si=phLOTljrb7v82kvv

New York Times. 2020. Eustachewich, Lia. How the Seattle CHOP zone went from socialist summer camp to deadly disaster. https://nypost.com/2020/07/01/how-seattle-chop-went-from-socialist-summer-camp-to-deadly-disaster/

Newsweek. 2020. Rahman, Khaleda. Black Lives Matter Chicago Organizer Defends Looting: 'That's Reparations'. https://www.newsweek.com/black-lives-matter-chicago-defends-looting-reparations-1524502

USA Today. 2021. Cox, Chelsey. Fact check: Quotes from Democratic leaders about riots, unrest taken out of context. https://www.usatoday.com/story/news/factcheck/2021/01/15/fact-check-quotes-democratic-leaders-riots-out-context/6588222002/

Fox 5 News. 2020. Baron, Julian. Black Lives Matter faces growing rift with local chapters over finances and transparency. https://foxbaltimore.com/news/nation-world/black-lives-matter-faces-rift-with-local-chapters-over-finances

New York Post. 2021. Brown, Lee. BLM leader says he quit after learning 'ugly truth' about group's priorities. https://nypost.com/2021/06/01/minneapolis-blm-leader-says-he-quit-after-learning-ugly-truth/

Associated Press. 2022. Melley, Brian. Mother: teachers manipulated child to change identity. https://apnews.com/article/business-california-gender-identity-cdb790cc3059e71e22d86b8e7b445361

CH. 9

Sidekick. No Date. Patel, Simon. How Governments and ISPs Can Monitor Your Internet Activity? https://www.meetsidekick.com/how-governments-and-isps-can-monitor-your-internet-activity/

The CATO Institute. 2021. Eddington, Patrick G. The PATRIOT Act Has Threatened Freedom for 20 Years. https://www.cato.

org/commentary/patriot-act-has-threatened-freedom-20-years?gad_source=1&gad_campaignid=85808169&gbraid=0AAAAADusmudXXxKTFB2i-waj9v9clFHYI&gclid=Cj0KCQjwxo_CBhDbARIsADWpDH5YX1K21GMexld9BG2-Vc-Y2RemTgrUSVG-YJypb2k_Al86DSnXWj4aApGGEALw_wcB

Texas Penal Codes. Title 7: Offenses Against Property. https://statutes.capitol.texas.gov/docs/pe/htm/pe.30.htm

CBS News. 2012. Tragedy At Fort Hood. https://www.cbsnews.com/feature/tragedy-at-fort-hood/

Inside Higher Ed. 2019. Grad School Activism. Grad School Activism. https://www.insidehighered.com/advice/2019/01/18/grad-school-activism-while-often-necessary-isnt-substitute-technic

Medium. 2016. Kuegler, Tom. I Had Zero Skills When I Graduated College. https://medium.com/the-post-grad-survival-guide/i-had-zero-skills-when-i-graduated-college-5334ae288ae4

CH. 10

Rumble. 2021. TECNTV.com / Is the Salvation Army WOKE Enough This Christmas? https://rumble.com/vq3kwr-tecntv.com-is-the-salvation-army-woke-enough-this-christmas.html

Wikipedia. 2025. The Largest Ship Building Companies. https://en.wikipedia.org/wiki/List_of_the_largest_shipbuilding_companies

Huffpost. 117th Congress. To reauthorize and amend the Magnuson-Stevens Fishery Conservation and Management Act, and for other purposes. https://huffman.house.gov/imo/media/doc/Sustaining%20America%27s%20Fisheries%20for%20the%20Future%20Act_Bill%20Text_7.26.2021.pdf

The Washington Post. 2014. Heim, Joe. Why is Christmas on the 25th of December, It Wasn't Always. https://www.washingtonpost.com/news/answer-sheet/wp/2014/12/24/why-is-christmas-on-dec-25-it-wasnt-always/

YouTube. 2020. Dr. Martin Luther King Jr. I have a Dream Speech—COLOR. https://www.youtube.com/watch?v=o8dzxh7Ybqw

YouTube. 2009. Rickey2b4. Morgan Freeman on Black History Month. https://www.youtube.com/watch?v=GeixtYS-P3s

New York Post. 2021. Chamberlain, Samuel. Hunter Biden repeatedly called his white lawyer the N-word, texts show. https://nypost.com/2021/06/08/hunter-biden-repeatedly-called-his-white-lawyer-the-n-word-texts-show/

Urban Dictionary. 2025. Nigga. https://www.urbandictionary.com/define.php?term=nigga

YouTube. 2017. Comedy Central. Chappelle's Show—The Niggar Family—Uncensored. https://www.youtube.com/watch?v=hLOw_SzkRQ8

People. 2020. Chung, Gabrielle. Howard Stern Addresses His Past Use of Blackface and N-Word: 'I Evolved and Changed'. https://people.com/tv/howard-stern-addresses-past-use-of-blackface-n-word/

Steven Shepard, "Democrats keep getting new warning signs about Black voter support", Politico, October 21, 2023, https://

www.politico.com/news/2023/10/21/democrats-black-voters-2024-00122846

YouTube. 2016. PlayNowPlayL8tr. Schoolhouse Rock—I'm Just a Bill. https://www.youtube.com/watch?v=OgVKvqTItto

Heritage Foundation. 2025 (2024). Election Fraud Map. https://electionfraud.heritage.org/search

The New Republic (TNR). 2022. Tannehill, Brynn. Why Elon Musk's Idea of "Free Speech" Will Help Ruin America. https://newrepublic.com/article/168309/elon-musk-twitter-free-speech-ruin-america

Heritage Foundation. 2025 (2024). Election Fraud Map. https://electionfraud.heritage.org/search

Hoover Institute. 2024. Volokh, Eugene, Bambauer, Jane, Mchangama, Jacob.Free Speech in European (and Other) Democracies, with Prof. Jacob Mchangama. https://www.hoover.org/research/free-speech-european-and-other-democracies-prof-jacob-mchangama

Instagram. 2022. Wiserebelfilms. Kanye West Interview. https://www.instagram.com/reel/Cj1CpS3on4L/?igshid=MDJmNzVkMjY%3D&fbclid=IwAR36he25dXNyKnA8F2SFefWSy-4ysq6hlftY5UTiU2gVHGjVgNYqe63U9J8

CBS Sports. 2022. Maloney, Jack. Kyrie Irving suspension: Jaylen Brown says NBPA has issues with requirements for Nets guard's reinstatement.https://www.cbssports.com/nba/news/kyrie-irving-suspension-jaylen-brown-says-nbpa-has-issues-with-requirements-for-nets-guards-reinstatement/

Amazon. 2018. Hebrews to Negroes: Wake Up Black America. https://www.amazon.com/Hebrews-Negroes-Wake-Black-America/dp/B07P5J2RR7

Sneaker News. 2022. Hernandez, Jovani. adidas To Sell Yeezy Footwear In 2023, Saves $302 Million Annually In Royalties Without Ye. https://sneakernews.com/2022/11/09/adidas-to-sell-rebranded-yeezy-2023/?fbclid=IwAR3EDAqMcdyxnfIdydWE4zkq8hbQuRWC-b9w243wDIu4y7gW693e51noet8

Stars and Stripes. 2017. Dickstein, Corey. More than a dozen Fort Hood soldiers arrested in Texas prostitution sting. https://www.stripes.com/news/more-than-a-dozen-fort-hood-soldiers-arrested-in-texas-prostitution-sting-1.486516

Center for Immigration Studies. 2016. Rush, Nayla. Somali Refugees in the US: Terrorist Have Families Too. https://cis.org/Rush/Somali-Refugees-US

Tallahassee Democrat. 2019. Somalian Resettlement Figures. https://data.tallahassee.com/refugee/alaska/somalia/all/

Reuters. 2017. Pantaleone, Wladimiro. Italy seizes NGO rescue boat for allegedly aiding illegal migration. https://www.reuters.com/article/us-europe-migrants-italy-ngo/italy-seizes-ngo-rescue-boat-for-allegedly-aiding-illegal-migration-idUSKBN1AI21B/

Research.com. 2025. Bouchrika, Imed. Number of College Graduates: 2025 Race, Gender, Age & State Statistics. https://research.com/universities-colleges/number-of-college-graduates#3

(*As appears in the original work*)

13 Soldiers Arrested in Prostitution Ring. 2017. https://www.stripes.com/news/more-than-a-dozen-fort-hood-soldiers-arrested-in-texas-prostitution-sting-1.486516

Rush, Nayla. 2016. Somali Refugees in the US: Terrorists Have Families Too. Center for Immigration Studies. https://cis.org/Rush/Somali-Refugees-US

Tallahassee Democrat. 2019. Somalian Resettlement Figures. https://data.tallahassee.com/refugee/alaska/somalia/all/

Pantaleone, Wladimiro. 2017. Italy Seizes NGO Rescue Boat for Allegedly Aiding in Illegal Immigration. Reuters. https://www.reuters.com/article/us-europe-migrants-italy-ngo/italy-seizes-ngo-rescue-boat-for-allegedly-aiding-illegal-migration-idUSKBN1AI21B

ACKNOWLEDGMENTS

FIRST, GIVING HONOR TO GOD and the Lord Jesus Christ for blessing me continually through the good and the bad times. I have always been a firm believer that "No weapon formed against me shall prosper, and I am more than a conqueror." (Isaiah 54:17 and Romans 8: 37, NKJV). Next, my family—not only by blood, but by relationship—you know who you are when I call you my family! Your continued support and encouragement in public and private motivate me every day. Friends, I thank you all as well. I use "friends" loosely, because friendship to me is based on mutual interest and respect, but I also have friends who only associate when it is in their interests. I am sure we all have those. Haters or lovers, I appreciate you all and thank you for your contributions to my life to make me who I am today and who I will grow to be. In my previous book, *The NEW You: Now Equipped with Wisdom: A Guide to Personal and Professional Development,* which I rushed through writing, I didn't give the proper respects and acknowledgments as I wanted to. However, I am making a concerted effort to do so now.

To my children, who keep me on my toes and grounded with their shenanigans. To my parents and stepparents, who continue to show their love for me even in my "old age." To my associates, colleagues, coworkers, business partners, and extended family members—far too many to mention, but most notably, Kenneth McClenton, whom I consider family: Thank you for your faith, encouragement, and words of wisdom in keeping me on track with TECN and in life; for putting a boot in my fourth-point-of-contact to get me started on writing this book. You are indeed a Godsend and have been a true blessing. To my colleagues at The Exceptional Conservative Network (TECN) and those over at Let The Truth Be Told Network: Thank you for all you do and for your support; you all mean a lot to me. To my colleagues and friends throughout the umbrella of the Republican Party of Texas and across the national and international political landscape: Thank you for your kindness, friendship, and all that you are doing in this great fight to save our REPUBLIC!

ABOUT THE AUTHOR

Photo by Heather Leider of Leider Photography

RANDY PURHAM WAS BORN AND raised in Chicago, Illinois, in 1980. He has a master's in political science from American Military University. He enlisted in the US Army in June 1998 and completed Basic Training and Advanced Individual Training at Fort McClellan, Alabama, as a Chemical Operations Specialist (74D). He has completed five campaigns in three tours in Iraq and one in Kuwait in support of Operation Enduring Freedom.

For over twenty-two years, he's been in a parallel career, as part of the multi-level marketing industry and as an independent business owner for various home-based businesses in his spare time. In 2013, he published his first book, *The NEW You: Now Equipped with Wisdom,* to help people who are seeking guidance in personal and professional development. He served as a member of the Ambassador Committee for the Anchorage Chamber of Commerce from 2012 to 2014 and was selected as a Gold Pan Finalist for Community Service as an individual. He also served as the junior vice commander of VFW Post 10252 during those same years.

From 2019 to 2020, he served as commander of VFW Post 12159—Naples, Italy, and District 1 commander, Department of Europe VFW, vice chairman for the Other Ranks Association—Joint Force Command Naples, all while serving as a CBRN advisor for NATO. Currently, he produces and hosts the web-based show, *Purham & Associates.*

Randy retired from the US Army in September 2020 and was a US congressional candidate for the state of Alaska. He now resides in Texas, where he does his show and political consulting under Purham & Associates, LLC. The personal philosophy behind everything he does is inspired by Zig Ziglar: "If you help enough people get everything they need, you'll have everything you need."